The Poor Man's Daughter

A Return to The Colleen Bawn

Published at www.lulu.com 2012

Our present subject might well have as title,
'The Failure to Pursue John Fitzgibbon Scanlan'

(Thomas Flanagan (1923-2002)
Author of *The Irish Novelists 1800-1850*)

Introduction

'I want to assure you that I die innocent'
(*Journals, Conversations and Essays relating to Ireland,* Nassau William Senior, London 1868, Vol II, 'Real History of the Colleen Bawn told by Lord Monteagle', pp173-177)

JOHN SCANLAN was hanged for the murder of Ellen Hanley on Thursday 16 March 1820 at Gallows Green in Limerick and his body given for dissection.[1] Four years later, a short story entitled *The Poor Man's Daughter* was published which alluded to the case.[2] Similar works followed, including Griffin's *Collegians*, and almost two hundred years on, the facts have been perverted by author, playwright and composer to produce the established myth of 'The Colleen Bawn'.[3]

The Poor Man's Daughter, reproduced here in its original form, is the forerunner of this literary evolution.

The identity of Scanlan remains obscure. William MacLysaght, author of *The Tragic Story of the Colleen Bawn* (1953), described this detail as 'not important to the story'.[4]

---

[1] *Ennis Chronicle and Clare Advertiser*, Sat 18 March 1820.

[2] *Tales of Irish Life* by Michael James Whitty, in two volumes, London 1824, 'The Poor Man's Daughter', Vol I, pp225-242.

[3] Appendix 1 (p27) is a chronology of works drawn on the murder. *The Collegians,* which followed Whitty's work, helped to establish Griffin's literary reputation.

[4] *Death Sails the Shannon: The Tragic [Authentic] Story of the Colleen Bawn the facts and the fiction* by William MacLysaght and Sigerson Clifford, Kerryman, Tralee, 1953 , p177. MacLysaght wrote, 'It is surprising how little is known of the Scanlan family'. This statement was dismissed in an article by Professor Thomas Flanagan, author of *The Irish Novelists 1800-1850,* as 'a little joke': 'A great deal can be discovered about this singular family, and without stirring from Dublin to consult neighbourhood oracles.... A properly detailed and thoughtful account of our present subject might well have as title, 'The Failure to pursue John Fitzgibbon Scanlan' (*Sunday Independent*, 27 October 1963, 'Mystery Still Cloaks our most famous murder').

Without identity, Scanlan's conviction has not been questioned.[5]

In failing to properly identify Scanlan, an accepted myth has prevailed.[6] It is evident from MacLysaght's research that Scanlan was a descendant of the Scanlan family of Ballynaha, Co Limerick, principal landowners of the period with noble associations. This information produces little impact today, but in 1819, the might of those connections was sufficient to keep the case out of the media.[7]

---

[5] Scanlan was represented at his trial by Daniel O'Connell, who wrote to his wife from Limerick, 15 March 1820: 'I had a client convicted yesterday for a murder for whom I fought a hard battle, and yet I do not feel any the most slight regret at his conviction. It is very unusual with me to be so satisfied, but he is a horrid villain .... He will be hanged tomorrow unless being a gentleman prevents him' (*The Field Day Anthology of Irish Writing*, Vol 1, p1130).

[6] Scanlan's family suppressed reporting of the case which resulted in the fusion of fact and fiction, and the challenge of separating the two is illustrated in the following accounts: 'John Scanlan lost his father in his infancy, and thus at an early age became the possessor of a handsome competency' (*Glasgow Herald*, 1 Feb 1862). '[*The Collegians*] was written in less than ten years after the murder was committed, when the parents of John Scanlan and those of Stephen Sullivan were still living' (*Nenagh Guardian*, 27 July 1892).

[7] 'Michael Scanlan was a near connection of Lord Clare, Lord Chancellor of Ireland' (*Irish Pedigrees, or The Origin and Stem of the Irish Nation* by John O'Hart, fifth edition, Vol II, Dublin 1892, p385). John Fitzgibbon, 1st Earl of Clare (1749-1802), was Lord Chancellor of Ireland 1789-1802. On his death the title passed to his son John, 2nd Earl of Clare, of Sidbury, Devon (1792-1851) who married but had no issue and the title passed to his brother, Colonel Richard Fitzgibbon, on whose death in 1864 the title became extinct. 'The foundation stone of Sarsfield bridge [Limerick] was laid 25th October 1824 by the Earl of Clare amidst great ceremony... the structure took eleven years to build and £89,000 was spent in its completion ...A statue standing on the bridge recalls that sinister figure in Irish history, John Fitzgibbon, Earl of Clare, whose part in bringing about the Union is never likely to be forgotten. It was to one of the last of his race however, the statue was erected, namely Viscount Fitzgibbon. Clare's son John died without issue. Colonel Richard Hobart Fitzgibbon succeeded his brother John. The latter's son, Viscount Fitzgibbon, was killed in the charge of Balaklava, and Richard Fitzgibbon, dying in 1864, the title became extinct. The statue is an exceedingly fine and graceful piece of work. The sculptor was Mr P Macdowall, RA, London' (*Irish Independent*, 22 March 1912).

Modern research methods have enabled a new approach to this case with wider access to relevant – if scant – material. As such, it is possible to construct a more precise account of the man tried for murder in 1819, one who 'undoubtedly neither married Ellen Hanly nor assisted in her murder'.[8]

John Scanlan was born c1797, the son of Matthew Scanlan Esq of Loghill and Catherine Cudmore of Ballycahane. Matthew Scanlan's father, Michael, was the lineal descendant of Scanlan, Kings of Ossory, and of antiquity.[9]

The parish of Loghill (or Loughill) in Limerick, situated on the banks of the river Shannon, contained land leased by the Scanlan family. Before and after his marriage, Matthew Scanlan was described as of this parish; it is probable that John Scanlan and his siblings were born there. The family may have resided at Hip Hall. Indeed, Scanlan is reputed to have sheltered there in the period before his arrest.[10]

---

[8] Conclusion of historian Mary Agnes Hickson (1825-1899), who examined 'every contemporary record and every printed account' of the case, including Judge Jebb's notebook, and who wrote, 'No one could write a true and impartial account of this celebrated crime unless he had examined all those written and printed old records most carefully, sifting and comparing them, and unless he had a thorough knowledge of the social, political and sectarian strifes and ambitions of certain parties in the County Limerick and the County Kerry between 1800 and 1817. Nor would even this suffice; he should have, in addition, a thorough knowledge of the blood relationships, clanships and personal characteristics of some of the persons who assisted in the prosecution of John Scanlan, and prevented even a brief respite being granted to the unfortunate youth ... and even when it was written, he or she would hesitate to print it at the present day lest the facts might give pain to inoffensive persons in different ranks of life whose immediate ancestors assisted in the prosecution and hurried execution of the unfortunate John Scanlan' (*Kerry Evening Post*, 19 September 1896).

[9] Documented and traced by genealogists in greatest detail from the early seventeenth century. See *Irish Pedigrees, or The Origin and Stem of the Irish Nation* by John O'Hart , fifth edition, Vol II, Dublin 1892, pp382-386, 'Scanlan Kings of Ossory' and *Irish Ancestor*, vol. 4, no. 2, 1972, pp71-80, 'Scanlan of the barony of Upper Connello, Co. Limerick' by Brian de Breffny and Alicia E. Evers.

[10] 'Scanlan of Ballycahane House, Croom was originally from Loughill and said to have stayed at Hip Hall in Carrowbane while on the run' (*Recollections of Our Native*

It is interesting to note that Gerald Griffin, whose novel *The Collegians* was based on this murder, resided at Fairy Lawn, in close proximity to Hip Hall.[11]

Matthew and Catherine Scanlan had five known children, John the eldest, the subject of this introduction; Anthony, captain of the *Hellas* and the *Sussex*;[12] Frances, who died a

---

Valley, a History of the Parish of Loughill-Ballyhahill and the Owvaun Valley by Gerald Curtin, published by Loughill-Ballyhahill Heritage Society, Limerick, 1996, p204). Matthew Scanlan is described in a memorial of deed of mortgage dated January 1809 as 'of Triphall' (Lysaght, p181); this would appear to be an error in transcription of Hip Hall. The Griffin family were later recorded at Hip Hall: 'Died Edward Griffin, second son of late John Griffin Esq of Hipham (*sic*) Limerick' (*Kerry Evening Post*, 30 July 1828). 'Feb 5, in Lower Hartstonge-street, Limerick, Ellen Maria Griffin, daughter of the late James Griffin Esq, Hip Hall, Co Limerick' (*Freeman's Journal*, 9 Feb 1865).

[11] It is commonly accepted that Griffin drew the material for his novel by acting as a courtroom reporter during the case. It is more likely that his knowledge derived from familiarity. In a letter to his brother in 1829, Griffin described how 'I am come home only this evening, wearied from steering the Hip Hall boat from Loughill to Pallas right before the wind' (*The Life of Gerald Griffin* by his brother, New York, second edition, 1857, p258). Of Griffin's *Collegians*, Kerry historian Mary Agnes Hickson wrote, 'Large allowance must be made for novelists and dramatists and all I shall say here of the novel of the *Collegians* is that it was a great pity that Gerald Griffin's undoubted talents should be employed in writing a work that, whatever amount of pecuniary profit or literary fame it brought to him, inflicted the deepest pain on a number of good, inoffensive and respectable families in his native county. It was written in less than ten years after the murder was committed, when the parents of John Scanlan and those of Stephen Sullivan, the actual murderer of the unhappy Ellen Hanly, were still living. Some remembrance of the deep truth contained in Lord Tennyson's lines might well have restrained Gerald Griffin's pen from selecting such a theme at such a time, when in the home of the gentleman and the peasant alike that truth found a sad echo: 'O children, there is nothing upon earth more miserable than she that hath a son and see him err' (*Nenagh Guardian*, 27 July 1892). Another near neighbour who composed a 'true history' was Rev Richard Fitzgerald of Ballydonohoe; see Appendix 1. An extract from this book is found in the *Kerry Evening Post*, 23 September 1896.

[12] Born c1800; married 26 February 1825 Isabella Henlon. Captained the passenger ship *Hellas* and clipper ship *Sussex*, 'First tea sale in Ireland. Friday the cargo of teas imported by Samuel Bewley and Sons, direct from Canton, per the *Hellas*, Captain Scanlan, was sold by auction at the Commercial-buildings' (*Morning Post*, 24 March 1835). 'The favourite and regular passenger ship *Sussex*, 1,000 tons, Captain Anthony Scanlan, is now on her way home from the Colony and will be again despatched for Melbourne' (*Reynolds Newspaper*, 17 May 1857). 'The *Sussex*, Captain Scanlan, 87 days from Melbourne, with over 48,000oz of gold, was off the [Plymouth] port this

bachelor;[13] and Michael, whose name was not mentioned in his father's legal affairs of 1839, suggesting he may have died before this date.[14] A daughter Elizabeth married Dr David McCullagh; she died young, and her husband died eleven years later in a bizarre accident when struck on the jugular vein by a cork.[15]

---

morning' (*The Standard*, 4 June 1857). 'Died 10th September, at 27 Wellington-square, Chelsea, Captain Anthony Scanlan, aged 68' (*The Standard*, 17 September 1868).

[13] 'A man named Scanlan, aged about 70 years, dropped dead the other day in Limerick. Scanlan's brother suffered the extreme penalty of the law about 50 years ago in connection with the Colleen Bawn trial' (*Liverpool Mercury*, 20 May 1869). 'Francis Scanlan, R.I.P. 02/05/1869 at North Strand, aged last birthday 60 years, a bachelor, his occupation was watchman or labourer. His cause of death was natural causes, suddenly, inquest' (information courtesy Eugene Canning, Registrar, Health Service Executive, St Camillus' Hospital, Limerick). 'Awfully sudden death in Limerick – A very sad occurrence took place yesterday between two and three o'clock on the Wellesley bridge road, Limerick, namely, the sudden death of a man named Francis Scanlan. When passing the toll-bar Scanlan stopped and paid his fare to the collector apparently in usual good health, and did not proceed thirty yards when he fell to the ground a lifeless corpse. He was of strictly sober habits, and attentive to business and connected with a family in this county whose reminiscences formed a leading feature in Griffin's *Collegians*, and now known to dramatic fans as the Colleen Bawn. It is said that Francis Scanlan, whose sudden death is now recorded, was nephew, and only surviving relative of Scanlan, executed 52 years ago at Gallows Green, in this city, for the murder (aided by Sullivan – 'Danny Man') of the unfortunate Eily O'Connor' (*Freeman's Journal*,13 May 1869).

[14] MacLysaght, p190.

[15] 'Died, Elizabeth McCullagh, wife of Dr David McCullagh, Assistant Surgeon, 84th Regiment' (*Kerry Evening Post*, 10 December 1831). 'On Tuesday last Dr McCullagh, late of the 84th Regiment, came by his death at Maghera, County Derry, in the following extraordinary manner: He and Dr Barr were about to drink off two bottles of soda water, and as Dr Barr was in the act of uncorking one, the cork flew out and struck Dr McCullagh on the jugular vein, who fell down and instantly expired' (*The Standard*, 19 December 1842). McCullagh in 1839 was described as 'David McCullagh of Maghera in the County of Londonderry Esq'. His assignee was Bridget Fogarty, Bruff, Co Limerick (MacLysaght, p190). In a letter from Bruff, Co Limerick addressed to Lord Lieutenant's Secretary, Dublin Castle (in which his name is spelt McCullough), McCullagh described his 'poor wife and three helpless children in a state of starvation'. He added, '[John Scanlan] I am sorry to say, is my brother-in-law. He was a second lieutenant of Marines, was dismissed the Service in the month of June 1815. After the murder of Ellen Henely (*sic*) – a young creature of 15 years old, whom he seduced, and took from her nearly £200, he went to Cork, after robbing and murdering her, and enlisted in Captain Chitty's company, 35th Regiment, from which regiment he deserted last October, was taken prisoner on 14th ult at his

Catherine Cudmore was the daughter of John Cudmore and Catherine Dalton of Ballycahane.[16] Ballycahane was evidently a grand residence but it was destroyed by fire in 1822.[17]

Accounts of Scanlan's arrest suggest a far more substantial building than the image purported to be Scanlan's residence in MacLysaght's publication.[18] Aubrey de Vere, a childhood friend of Gerald Griffin, described the capture of John Scanlan as given to him by the captor, a magistrate and 'near relative'. A body of police had arrived at Ballycahane at a late hour of night when a dinner-party was in progress

> He was received in the hall by its mistress, a tall and stately lady in a black velvet dress. She addressed him with quiet scorn, informed him that her house, a hospitable one, had been favoured by many guests, but none resembling those who had come at that unusual hour to visit it; that she knew his errand; that her son had not been in that house for many weeks; but that he was welcome to search for him as he pleased.[19]

---

father's, Ballycahane Castle, in this county' (MacLysaght, p172). Capt Charles Chitty was officer of 35th Regiment of Foot from 2nd July 1818 to 12 Oct 1820. 'The regiment landed at Cork on 4th January [1819] where it went into quarters.... On the 30th June 1820 the regiment left Cork for Waterford (*An Historical Memoir of the 35th Royal Sussex Regiment of Foot* Compiled by Richard Trimen, late Captain 35th Foot, Southampton: 1873, p188 & pp121-122).

[16] 'This morning a duel was fought at Kilpecan, between R_d M_ll, junior, and M_l S_n, Esqs, when after discharging a pistol each, they were parted by the interposition of Joseph Crips Esq and Capt Cudmore' (*Gazeteer*, 1 August 1764).

[17] 'Limerick March 2 – the extensive buildings of Ballycahane House and Offices were totally consumed last night by the insurgents, who previously removed the horses – the house was fortunately unoccupied; Ballycahane is the estate of George Leake Esq and is situated within six miles of this city. We are informed that the party who committed this outrage amounted to 300, and they placed centinels (*sic*) on the houses of Mr Leake's tenantry, to prevent them rendering any assistance in suppressing the fire – nothing but the walls of the Mansion remain' (*Freeman's Journal*, 5 March 1822). 'March & April 1822: George Leake, magistrate, County Limerick, complained to William H Gregory, Under Secretary of Ireland, Dublin Castle, of financial losses especially destruction by rebels of house and offices at Ballycahane' (National Archives of Ireland, Ref: CSO/RP/1822/649).

[18] MacLysaght; image facing p64. This photograph of Ballycahane is perhaps a rebuild, or a surviving building converted into a residence. It was demolished in the 1970s.

[19] *Recollections of Aubrey de Vere*, London 1897, pp28-29.

On the subsequent discovery of Scanlan in an outhouse, 'the magistrate told me that the most terrible thing he had ever witnessed was the contrast between that mother's stately bearing at first and the piteous abjectness of her later appeals as, on her knees, she implored him to spare her son'.[20]

The deaths of Matthew Scanlan Esq and Catherine Scanlan were recorded in 1840 and 1832 respectively.[21] Of their son John, there are only questions: How did he conduct his short life? Was he a first lieutenant of marines, or a second lieutenant, as claimed by McCullagh? Was he the dark character he is portrayed, or a young gentleman of wealth and

---

[20] *Ibid.* Another version of the arrest was given by Lord Monteagle in 1862, as recounted by Nassau William Senior: 'I knocked at the door and asked for Mr Scanlan, the father. A minute or so passed, during which there seemed to be some disturbance within; and I was ushered into a room in which some of the family were seated by the fire. I said that I had come on a painful duty – to execute a warrant against their son. 'You' screamed the mother. 'You a Rice come to arrest a Scanlan! There is equally pure blood in both our veins'. Following the arrest, Scanlan sent for Lord Monteagle: 'He sent to beg me to visit him in his cell. When I entered he said: 'I sent for you in the first place to tell you that I bear you no ill-will. You did only your duty. And secondly, I want to assure you that I die innocent. I did not kill Eily O'Connor. How was it possible that wooing her as I had done, I could have harmed her? Sullivan instead of putting her as he had agreed, on board an American vessel, stunned her with the musket butt end, and then threw her into the Shannon. As a proof of the truth of my story you will find the musket hid in the cave under the promontory from whence the boat started' (*Journals, Conversations and Essays relating to Ireland* by Nassau William Senior in two volumes; London 1868; Vol II, 'Real History of the Colleen Bawn told by Lord Monteagle [1 Oct 1862]', pp173-177). Same account reproduced in *Limerick Christmas Gazette* No 3, 1989, p26. It will be observed in this account that by 1868, Ellen Hanley's identity had altered to her fictional 'Eily O'Connor'. Note also a third version of Scanlan's arrest claimed he was apprehended at 'the residence of Mr M____ of S____, one of the most independent and influential men in the county of Limerick' (*Recollections of an Irish Police Magistrate*, p147; refer to appendix 1 for details). This may have referred to Mr Massy of Stagdale. Elizabeth Scanlan of Ballynaha, Scanlan's aunt, had married in 1792 Hon George Massy of Stagdale Lodge, Co Limerick.

[21] 'At his house at the Strand, last Saturday [6th], Mathew Scanlan Esq, son of the late Michael Scanlan of Ballinaha Esq in this county and brother-in-law to the Hon George Eyre Massy' (*Limerick Chronicle*, 10 June 1840). 'Died, Catherine Scanlan, wife of Matthew Scanlan of Ballycahane' (*Kerry Evening Post*, 27 June 1832). Burial places not known.

leisure hoodwinked by an older and unscrupulous boatman?[22] Did he exploit Ellen Hanley, or love her? Was he under pressure from his family to commit to an arranged union? Did he plan Ellen Hanley's transportation, or her murder? Was Ellen Hanley murdered? Can a corpse in an advanced state of decay be identified by a tooth socket? In the absence of a published account of Scanlan's trial, the questions remain.

Scanlan protested his innocence to the end. Historian Mary Agnes Hickson, who studied the case in contemporary records, had no doubt that his was a 'mistaken sentence', and alluded to the sacrificial.[23] She maintained that the history of his conviction, hampered by 'falsehoods' and 'catchpenny narratives', could not be assessed without a thorough knowledge of the social, political and sectarian conditions in Limerick and Kerry between 1800 and 1817 and an understanding of the blood relationships, clanships and personal characteristics of those who assisted in the prosecution and prevented Scanlan 'even a brief respite'.[24]

---

[22] Lady Morgan described Scanlan as 'dissipated' following a conversation about the murder with William Henry Curran: 'His uncle, Mr Scanlan, was High Sheriff last year; Curran dined with him the day of the hero's execution. Curran said the uncle's *sang froid* and indifference were frightful; he shrugged his shoulders, tucked his napkin under his chin, said 'it was a sad business' and called for soup' (*Lady Morgan's Memoirs: Autobiography, Diaries and Correspondence*, Vol II, London, 1862, pp288-290). She concluded, 'Scanlan had been condemned on the strongest circumstantial evidence'.

[23] *Nenagh Guardian*, 27 July 1892. 'Justice, good faith, truth, common honesty, Christian charity go down before this spirit of party. Its worship is virtually as cruel, treacherous and devilish in this nineteenth century after Christ as ever was the worship of Baal and Moloch' (*Kerry Evening Post*, 19 September 1896).

[24] *Nenagh Guardian*, 27 July 1892. 'The junior branch of the Scanlan family of Limerick county, to which the unhappy youth belonged, is long extinct, and the statement that he ever was the heir of the owners of Ballynaha and Ballyknockane, High Sheriffs of Limerick County in 1796 and 1826, is one of the many falsehoods with which those catchpenny narratives are filled'.

On the day of his execution, Scanlan was taken from Limerick prison in a carriage escorted by a prison guard and Rev Henry Gubbins, garrison chaplain at Limerick:[25]

> At a distance of a few hundred yards from the gaol, a bridge was to be passed. The horses, which had shown no signs of restiveness before ... came to a full stop ... every effort to get the carriage forward failed, the prisoner was removed from it, and conducted on foot to the place of execution. It was a solemn and melancholy sight as he slowly moved along the main street of a crowded city, environed by military, unpitied by the populace, and gazed at with shuddering curiosity from every window[26]

---

[25] Rev Gubbins later stated that Scanlan 'suffered for a crime in which he did not participate' (*Kerry Evening Post*, 16 September 1896). Rev Gubbins was born in Limerick c1786, son of James Gubbins of Kenmare Castle, Co Limerick by his second wife. Curate St Mary's, Limerick from 1812, rector and vicar Kilcolman 1816-45, vicar Kilmoylan 1824-45, vicar choral Limerick 1829-45, vicar Clonelty 1840-45, garrison chaplain at Limerick. He married on 3 November 1810 Avarina, daughter of Cpt Robert Atkins of Fountainville, Co Cork and had issue Robert Atkins, Lieut 62nd regt, killed at Sutlej 24 December 1845 unmarried; Rev Henry Gubbins, curate Dromtariffe, Co Cork; Sarah, who married son of Roger O'Callaghan; Avarina and Letitia. Rev Gubbins died suddenly 22 August 1845: 'Rev Henry Gubbins, curate of St Mary's parish and vicar of Kilbreedy, Limerick died suddenly on Friday. The rev gentleman was returning as usual from daily morning service at the Cathedral and on foot, manifestly in good health, without any complaint of indisposition, when he suddenly staggered against the iron railing of the Scottish Union Insurance Office, George-street, and was falling on the flag-way when Mr Frost, one of the union guardians, who walked behind, caught him in his arms and asked how he felt to which the rev gentleman faintly answered that he was better, and it would not signify. He then inquired for his hat, which had fallen into the area, and Mr Frost assisted him into the office, where he sat on a form until the hat was brought up, and was just rising to proceed home when the angel of death dealt the fatal blow to his victim and the rev gentleman sunk exhausted upon the steps, almost without a struggle, and after two or three convulsive throes of the breast, finally resigned his spirit with scarce an audible sigh. Thus died the rev Henry Gubbins, well known and gratefully acknowledged by all classes of people as one of the laborious 'working clergy' of the diocese, at all times and seasons, and for at least a period of 35 years' (*The Standard*, 26 August 1845).

[26] *The New Monthly Magazine*, 1825, pp506-8; see appendix 1 for full reference. 'Baal's Bridge, the origin or whose name man knoweth not now, had at one time houses and shops on it, as was often the fashion in ancient cities. It connects the Englishtown with the Irishtown, and it was over its predecessor that John Scanlan, the murderer of Ellen Hanley, 'The Colleen Bawn' was conveyed from the old prison in the Englishtown for execution on Gallows Hill' (*Irish Independent*, 22 March 1912).

Scanlan was unsteady, evidently from the effects of laudanum:

> Without the assistance of the gaoler and clergyman who supported him between them, he must, to all appearance, have dropped on the pavement[27]

At the scaffold, Rev Gubbins offered Scanlan the opportunity to confess to which he replied, 'I am suffering for a crime in which I never participated; if Sullivan is ever found, my innocence will appear'.[28] Soon after, 'a lash was given to the horse' to 'launch Scanlan into eternity'.[29]

The figure of John Scanlan remains in the shadows. From this distance, it can be said that in silencing the press, Scanlan's family succeeded in protecting their son – and their family name – from a world that knows little more now than two centuries ago.

Hickson described Scanlan's execution as 'hurried'.[30] In the same year that the body alleged to be that of Ellen Hanley was washed up on the banks of the Shannon, a case of abduction of a young woman from the same area was heard in court. The matter was brought to the attention of the press courtesy of

---

[27] *The New Monthly Magazine*, 1825, pp506-8.

[28] *Ibid.* This account was also published in Lenihan's history of Limerick, who on recounting Scanlan's last words, added, 'He thus died with a lie in his mouth' (*Limerick: its History and Antiquities, Ecclesiastical, Civil and Military from the Earliest Ages* by Maurice Lenihan Esq, Dublin 1866, pp450-454). Stephen Sullivan was arrested four months after Scanlan's execution, and tried and convicted of the murder of Ellen Hanley. He was executed on 27 August 1820 and his body given for dissection. Shortly before he made a full confession. Sullivan's trial was widely reported: *The Examiner*, 6 August 1820; *Caledonian Mercury*, 14 August 1820; *Glasgow Herald*, 14 August 1820; *Freeman's Journal*, 1 August 1820. See also 'The Colleen Bawn, The True History of her Case' by H M Jebb, *Kerry Evening Post*, 16 September 1896 and *The true story of the Colleen* Bawn, Kevin Grattan, *Maigueside Journal*, 1998, pp45-48.

[29] MacLysaght, p155.

[30] *Nenagh Guardian*, 27 July 1892.

'the friend of the oppressed', who hinted at 'a traffic in human blood'.[31] The timing and outcome of Scanlan's romance may have meant that, unfortunately for him, there was more at stake than the good name of his family.

Researched and produced by
Janet Murphy and Eileen Chamberlain
Killarney & UK
August 2012

Illustrations
Front cover image: From an original painting by John Reidy, Castleisland, Co Kerry
Back cover image: All that remains of Ballynaha, Co Limerick

---

[31] *Caledonian Mercury*, 16 August 1819, 'Prosecution of a Magistrate': 'The girl was accused of being intimate with a man, whose wife had sufficient influence, through others, to induce this modern Nero to inflict summary punishment on the object of their vengeance ... I call it a traffic in human blood'. Article also published in *The Annual Register, or a View of the History, Politics and Literature for the year 1819*, London: 1820. William Borough Esq and John Magrath were tried in 1819 at the Record Court before Baron Smith for conspiring to transport a woman named Judith Lynch to America. It was alleged that the woman was taken from her father's house at Clarefield in Limerick and 'actually put on board of a vessel then under sail with passengers for America; that she was actually taken to America, and brought back by order and at the expense of government'. The accused were convicted, 'this prosecution shows clearly that no man of any rank is permitted to trample upon the liberties of the meanest subject in the realm' (*Freeman's Journal*, 3 August 1819). A number of documents are held at the Chief Secretary's Office Registered Papers (National Archives of Ireland) in relation to this subject, see CSO/RP/1818/440/20; CSO/RP/1818/531; CSO/RP/1819/112; CSO/RP/1819/590; CSO/RP/SC/1821/1476. In document CSO/RP/1819/590, Lynch expresses her gratitude for 'bringing her home from America to prosecute Mr Borough' and looks for assistance 'being in the last stage of pregnancy'. On the subject of transportation, Hickson wrote of Sullivan, 'Instead of putting [Hanley] on board an emigrant ship from Kilkee to America, as he had been engaged to do, he preferred murdering her and seizing her money and clothes' (*Kerry Evening Post*, 19 September 1896). See also Addison's account, 'Lest Scanlan might legally marry her, his family had insisted on his sending her off to America' (p144). Reference at Appendix 1.

The Poor Man's Daughter

Women are frail too,
Ay, as the glasses where they view themselves,
Which are as easy broke as they make forms.
Women! help Heaven! men their creation mar
In profiting by them. SHAKSPEARE

ON the right hand side of the road from Kilrush to Clare lie the ruins of a poor cottage, which was lately inhabited by a peasant, who enjoyed the singular felicity of being contented with the gifts which Fortune had bestowed upon him. This poor but honest man exemplified daily the compatibility of divine and moral laws; for whilst, in the field, he endured the 'penalty of Adam,' he was never known to act contrarily to the most rigid integrity, always blessing Heaven for his share of worldly things, and never repining because he saw profusion bestowed upon others less grateful. The Christian, who is taught to expect rewards hereafter, is not always so purified from terrestrial hopes as not to retain much of the Israelites' creed in anticipating some manifestation of Heaven: perhaps it is only the vanity of human nature which increases the value of possessions by attributing them to Divine interposition; or it may be owing to the exaggeration of partiality, which sets such an exorbitant value on the gift, that nothing less than Omnipotence could bestow it: certain it is we are either willing to flatter ourselves by an indirect approval of our conduct, or we endeavour to account for that which is enveloped in mystery by acknowledging 'all is of God.' This poor man's possessions were few, but these were of great value to him: his health enabled him to live independently of absolute want, and his daughter Sally endeared him to that life which he laboured to prolong. These two gifts (for such he called them) were to him such a blessing and such a happiness, that his gratitude to Heaven was incessant, being his first acknowledgment in the morning, and the last in the evening; and so intertwined were both with his existence, that the loss of one would have destroyed his enjoyment of the other.

Beauty is the gift of Nature; and, as equal care is bestowed on the formation of all, it is no wonder that the daughters of Poverty are sometimes handsome. Sally was one of those perfect figures which could only be conceived by the genius of Phidias, but never could be portrayed by the chisel of a statuary; nor did the beauty of her face lessen the admiration which her form excited, being at once intelligent, animated, and lovely. Sally was blessed by the aged, and beloved by the youthful; and so docile was her disposition, and so unaffected her manners, that envy was found nowhere to lessen the general esteem in which she was held; whilst the absence of vicious greatness from that part of the country awakened no apprehension that guilt would be allured to the destruction of virtue, beauty, and innocence. Every blessing brings with it something to detract from human happiness, on the same principle that no metal is found unaccompanied by alloy; and, were not many evils entailed upon Ireland by the wilful expatriation of the aristocracy, their absence might be pardoned for the security which it affords to unsuspecting virtue. If the non-existence of crime be a proof of innocence, the Irish peasantry are entitled to the praise of enviable morality; for cases of seduction are seldom known among them, whilst the incontinent are disallowed, by public reprobation, to consort with society.

Sally, accustomed to playmates innocent as herself, apprehended no evil from associating with those who, though now growing fast to manhood, were once her school-fellows; and, being ignorant of the nature of crime, her conduct was not regulated by any fears of indiscretion: she was seen joyful in the harvest-field, where her sex are found, in Ireland, gladdening the reaper's toil; and on the farmer's floor her smile dispensed pleasure among her companions, whether spinning or quilting. Sally's cheerfulness of temper was so well known, and her simple powers of pleasing so well acknowledged, that she was never unemployed, as all were eager to have her in the family. The little sums thus acquired by laudable industry she regularly deposited in her father's hand, whose approving kiss was the best reward of duty: she knew her father was poor, and this knowledge regulated her economy. When going to market with eggs or poultry, she saved her Sunday shoes by walking within a mile of the town barefooted,* and kept every gown twelve months before she put in on of a week-day: the superfluity of a new-patterned handkerchief was purchased by the labour of after-hours; and one riband cost her the minute savings of six months. Nor was her father less laboriously careful: he often walked three miles a day to work for sixpence; and, when even that could not be procured, his little field behind his hut was prepared for the future supply of potatoes. The reward of industry was evident in the poor man's cottage: one room was filled with an annual supply of the national esculent, and the little white dresser had many rows of variegated delf; whilst warm clothes were worn by the old man, and neat ones by his daughter every Sunday at chapel. As Sally approached her eighteenth year, it is not to be supposed she wanted admirers: many paid her attention,

* Notwithstanding the privations of the peasantry in Ireland, no people possess a greater desire for decency. The following extract from 'A Report of the present State of the disturbed Districts in the South of Ireland' the author knows to be candid and true: 'They are so much attached to dress, that they would deprive themselves of sufficient food, and live on one meal of potatoes in the day, without complaint, to obtain good clothing: their being in rags, therefore, is a strong indication of extreme misery. They are exceedingly partial to shoes and stockings, the want of which they consider a degradation: those who find difficulty in procuring them seldom wear any, except on holidays and Sundays; and, in travelling, carry them in their hands, for the sake of economy, and of having their feet unconfined on the journey. The women travel to chapel and to fairs on the same principle until they get near their destination, when they stop at a stream to wash their feet, and put them on.'

but her preference distinguished a youth who was serving his time to a rustic carpenter. This lad had given so many proofs of industry and application to his business, that the old man readily consented to his being admitted as Sally's future husband. Tom O'Driscoll (this young man's name) anticipated so much felicity in the society of Sally, when religion had sanctioned their union, that he waited with impatience for the expiration of his apprenticeship; but, as he was to live by labour, he could not be too soon industrious: he therefore employed his leisure hours in preparing for housekeeping by making half a dozen oak chairs, two tables, and a bedstead. Sally admired this proof of his wishes to make her happy, and cheered the drooping age of her father by sly insinuations of the cradle; and more than once, by studied mistake, called him grandfather. Happiness was visible in the poor man's countenance as the idea of seeing himself perpetuated in a future race darted into his face – like the flash of sunbeams on a dilapidated ruin, making decay more apparent.

Thus the old man continued to be happy, and the young people lived in anticipation of their future felicity, when a stranger one day stepped into the cottage where Sally was spinning, and asked for a drink of water, which was given him, not without many apologies for not having something better. The day being warm, the stranger prolonged his stay, under the pretence of resting, whilst he insidiously was profiting by the inexperience of this unsuspecting girl, collecting from her candid answers the history of her circumstances; and, on his going away, slipped into her hand a note, whilst his quick departure prevented her from returning the undeserved remuneration for a seat and a drink of water. Money has charms for all: even those who are unable to resist it, when surreptitiously offered, are always ingenious in fabricating excuses for retaining it. Sally, after a moment's doubt, concluded her visitor was one of those amiable characters mentioned in fairy tales, who 'do good by stealthy, and blush to find it fame.' His liberality was evident, whilst his motive could not but be pure, as he was neither displeasingly familiar nor known in the country. She never expected to see him again, as he did not promise to return. These thoughts were dissipated by the entrance of a travelling pedlar, who, spreading out his wares, succeeded in tempting Sally to become a purchaser of garters, ribands, scissors, and pins, for which she paid with the stranger's note; but no sooner was the itinerant merchant gone that a difficulty arose in her mind that she could not overcome but by concealment: her father was to remain ignorant of the transaction, not so much from a fear of his anger, as that it should give him trouble; for he had sometimes lately dwelt on the danger of girls accepting presents from men, particularly from those whose superior station in life precluded any degree of intimacy.

Sally was the next day at her usual task, when, at the same hour as before, the stranger made his appearance: a better dress and greater confidence were the only difference she could perceive. As he told her he was then on his return homewards, it seemed to account for his second visit; and, as he kissed her cheek on going away, she thought there was no occasion to be angry, the gentleman being young and handsome. To Sally's surprise he came the next day, bringing with him a silk handkerchief, which he familiarly tied round her neck; and, on her signifying her displeasure by a repulse, he fell on his knees, whilst, in terms the most passionate, he declared his love, calling heaven and earth to witness his honourable intentions: acknowledging her beauty, he indignantly spurned the idea of hiding such excellence in retirement, telling her, as he tumultuously kissed her hand, that he had rank and fortune to bestow upon her the moment she would honour him with her heart. The high and cultivated have been found too weak in resisting the seducer's art: no wonder, then, that simple girls have been insnared. Sally, on hearing the compliments bestowed upon her, examined her glass, and believed herself handsome: whilst the earnestness of her admirer appeared like sincerity, his gentlemanly appearance and refined address gained upon her heart, until at length she consented to become his bride.

The evening fixed on for her departure from her father's cottage was early in the month of May; and, as it approached, she regarded it not without dread. Her lover might be false, and the bare possibility of his being so was sufficient to awaken the keenest apprehension: but his promises were fair, and she relied upon them and the strength of her own virtue. The evening came, and, as if it were to be the last, her rustic lover paid her a visit: a few days were to terminate his servitude, when the whole of his acquired and created property was to be removed to his wife's abode, and this evening himself and the old man were regulating how they should dispose of it. Several times he inquired if Sally was ill, she looked so dejected; and several times he pressed her hand, to give her courage to overcome what he thought were maiden apprehensions. Never was he happier than on his departure that night; for Sally, knowing he was deceived, though he was still dear to her, gave him an ardent kiss, which, if interpreted rightly, said, 'This is the last.' At length the hour came: Sally was ready; and, taking farewell of her unconscious and sleeping father, joined her lover, who quickly conveyed her to Ennis, where she had courage enough to demand the fulfilment of his promise. Her lover knew he had conquered her heart, but he dared not venture to invade her virtue: to satisfy her, and escape, as he thought, with impunity, he took her to a rejected priest, significantly called, in Ireland, '*Tack-em*,' where the ceremony was performed;

but, when concluded, the clergyman required, as well as his fee, the bridegroom's signature, acknowledging his marriage, at the same time handing Sally her certificate. Often are the protections of virtue mysteriously evinced: this villain thought the unfortunate priest was too ignorant and too wicked to note the marriage; and the surprise of the unexpected discovery of his error so confounded him, that, in the confusion of his own ideas, he signed the book 'Richard M'Naughton.'

'The birth of the crime,' says an eloquent orator, speaking of seduction, 'is the death of enjoyment:' M'Naughton was no sooner satiated with the company of his wife than he wished to be freed from her. Her innocent appeals to his love were tiresome; her affectionate fondness was troublesome. He took her to Killarney, under the pretence of amusement; settled in a neat cottage; and bought a boat, for the purpose of sailing on its delightful lakes. Here he lived from all society but that of Sally and a confidential man – apparently kind, but often dejected and gloomy. One evening he pretended business to the next town, desiring his man to amuse his mistress by sailing on the waters, which impart a thousand beauties to the islands and hills of Killarney. Sally, all confidence, apprehended no danger, but was surprised in the evening to find her husband, on his return, outrageously turbulent, directing all his anger towards his devoted servant, whilst the cause was as unknown to her as this conduct was inexplicable.

The next evening M'Naughton, accompanied by Sally and his man, went on the lakes as usual. It was in the midst of summer: all Nature rejoiced in the beauties of creation, and romantic loveliness every way met the gazer's eye, whilst his ears were feasted with the melody of a thousand echoes, reciprocally repeated from dell and hill. Every valley was an undulated expanse of water; and from every rock tumbled, in harmonious cadence, a natural cascade. Yet, enchanting as all around really was, Sally was the loveliest object which the sun then illumined: her heart, attuned by innocent gaiety to the charms of every beauteous scene, was this evening full of the sublime imagery which the hand of Nature has here unsparingly pictured; and, as if the conceptions of the soul were delineated in the features, Sally's face showed an accordant sublimity with what her eyes beheld. Cursed ambition! thy withering maledictions blast the fair impressions of virtuous beauty, and blind thy votaries to the pleasure of sublime conceptions: no object is too lovely to escape immolation on thy guilty altar; and no crime too heinous, when the perpetration is to facilitate an admission to thy rewards. Poor Sally fell a sacrifice to thy atrocious spirit!

The father of Sally, and her betrothed husband, O'Driscoll, alarmed by the flight of the common object of their affections, pursued her, with unceasing solicitude, from town to town, and had on this evening arrived in Killarney, where they got intelligence of Sally's retreat. On going to the cottage they discovered that herself and paramour were in the boat on the lake: glad of once more having the prospect of beholding his child, the old man, supported by O'Driscoll, clambered over rock and hill until they got a view of the boat as it drifted along with the current of the water. The sight of the poor man's child drew from his reverend eyes a flood of tears; nor could O'Driscoll refrain from weeping as he vowed revenge on her seducer. For some time they could view the easy progress of the boat; but a turn in the lake, and an intervening hill, hid it from their sight, when presently they heard a dreadful scream; another – and another – fainter and fainter. A thousand fears for Sally rushed upon her father, who, gaining the summit of the hill, saw, immediately under him, the dead body of his child cast into the water, where it instantly sunk. 'Murderous villains!' he exclaimed, and fell into O'Driscoll's arms.

On recovering, the old man directed O'Driscoll to look down the precipice, but all there was silent: on the opposite side of the lake they saw the boat without any one in it. 'Alas!' said the poor man, 'we came one hour too late to save Sally from destruction; but let us secure her body, and lay it beside her mother, where I now wish to be laid myself.' The town where they went for assistance was not far off: the people came in crowds to see if such imputed atrocity was true, and could not be convinced until the body of Sally was dragged on shore, mutilated and disfigured. A general sensation of horror was spread through the country, and the fearless conduct of one youthful magistrate apprehended the murderer, M'Naughton, who, it appeared, was allied to some families of the highest respectability in Ireland, whose interest with the executive was so powerful, that the judge who tried him, acting in a manner which would have immortalized a Roman, ordered his immediate execution lest a reprieve might be obtained.

Twelve months after, the guilty servant of M'Naughton was tried and convicted: before execution he confessed that his master was on the eve of being married to a young lady of fortune, provided by his sister; and that, fearing the claim of Sally might be substantiated, he resolved to murder her. For this purpose he made his man provide a large club, a heavy stone to tie to the corse (*sic*) for sinking it, and sent him out with her to perform the deed singly: 'but,' said the culprit, 'as I raised the club in a threatening manner, she, thinking I was only frightening her, gave me a smile so sweet and innocent that I could not strike.' For this his master was displeased on the last night of Sally's existence; he having the next evening perpetrated the murder himself.

Virtue is most lovely when it comes in a pleasing form; and murder, however dreadful, is seen with aggravated horror when youth and beauty are the victims. The impression made in Ireland by the fate of Sally is still fresh in the memory of all. The old recite her history for its example to credulous maids and the young listen to it because it is romantic and strange: its truth is too well attested to be doubted, and the criminal records of the country retain the particulars of the atrocious transaction. The father of Sally soon joined the remains of his injured daughter; and O'Driscoll never passes the ruins of the cottage without praying for their repose, laying the emphasis of invocation on the name of Sally, the anniversary of whose death is yet remembered by her former companions, who on that fatal day, strew her green grave with friendly-woven wreaths of many-scented flowers – votive offerings of pure esteem to the memory of the hapless woman who lies beneath.

Tales of Irish Life illustrative of the Manners, Customs and Condition of the People with designs by George Cruickshank by Michael J Whitty, in two volumes, London 1824; 'The poor Man's Daughter', Vol I, pp225-242.

Appendix 1: Chronology of works drawn on the murder

1824

Tales of Irish Life by Michael James Whitty, in two volumes, London 1824, 'The poor Man's Daughter', Vol I, pp225-242. Whitty (c1795-1873) was born in Wexford c1795, he moved to London 1821 and was appointed editor of the *London and Dublin Magazine* in 1823. From 1829 until his death in 1873 he lived and worked in Liverpool. Whitty would appear to be the first to publish a fictionalised account of the affair.

1825

The New Monthly Magazine and Literary Journal, No LX, Vol X, Boston, 1825, pp497-508. Subsequently republished with footnotes in *Sketches of the Irish Bar* by the Rt Hon Richard Lalor Shiel, MP, with memoir and notes by R Shelton Mackenzie, DCL, in two volumes; Redfield, New York: 1854, Vol I, pp42-57 (in which Mackenzie put forward a conspiracy theory: 'There are yet hundreds in the county of Limerick who were present at this execution, and seriously believed that it was not Mr Scanlan who was hanged, but some other prisoner who was rendered unconscious by means of strong narcotics', p57) and in *Sketches of the Irish Bar; with Essays, Literary and Political* by William Henry Curran Esq, London, 1855, Vol I, pp297-324.

1828

The Collegians by Gerald Griffin in three volumes first published c1828, 'The second edition of the popular novel of *The Collegians* will be published Monday next' (*The Standard*, 25 July 1829). A short study of Griffin by Thomas Flanagan concluded that unlike other novelists of the period, Griffin wrote 'without condescension' and that 'through his anecdotes, rambling and seemingly inconsequential, we learn the history of the intertwined Limerick families' (*The Irish Novelists 1800-1850*, New York and London, 1959, pp203-251; citation p229). Flanagan suggested that Griffin in his *Collegians* 'had not written a novel about Ireland; he had written an Irish novel'. The Ireland of *The Collegians* 'simply exists' (p230). In the same study he remarked, 'The absence of law is at the center of every story which Griffin was to write' (p214).

1831

Eily O'Connor; or, The Foster Brother. 'The first stage version of Griffin's Collegians was made by Thomas Egerton Wilkes as *Eily O'Connor; or, The Foster Brother* and performed at the City Theatre London in July 1831 (*Morning Post*, 25 July 1831 & *The Era*, 8 February 1896).

1840/41
Colleen Bawn and Colleen Dhu, Samuel Lover's 1840 artwork, was publicised; the name was applied to a horse raced by Lord Milltown in 1845.

1860
The Colleen Bawn or The Brides of Garryowen: a Domestic Drama in Three Acts by Dion Boucicault opened New York March 1860 at Laura Keene's Theatre (film versions were subsequently made including one filmed in Ireland by Kalem Film Company and produced in 1911). 'Mr Dion Boucicault, while playing Myles-na-Coppaleen in the Colleen Bawn at the Crystal Palace met with a severe accident on Monday evening in making the jump to save Eily O'Connor from drowning. Mr Boucicault was unable to proceed with his part' (*York Herald*, 13 July 1881). Queen Victoria enjoyed Boucicault's play to such an extent that watercolourist Egron Sellif Lundgren (1815-1875) was commissioned to paint a series of scenes from the play.

1860
The Lost Bride of Garryowen, or, St Patrick's Eve by Charles H Horsman (1825-1886). Drama in two acts for performance at Queen's, Manchester. Perpetual injunction granted to restrain the production following proceedings by Boucicault (above) alleging plagiarism. An aggrieved Horsman described Boucicault as 'self important': 'Does his success give him the sole and undivided right to dramatise Griffin's work?' (*The Era*, 11 Nov 1860). Horsman was married to actress Charlotte Gardiner in 1847, whose death was reported in *The Era*, 9 June 1878.

1860
Eily O'Connor, drama in two acts by C H Hazlewood, licensed for performance at the Britannia.

c1861
Miss Eily O'Connor. A New and Original Burlesque founded on the Great Sensation Drama of The Colleen Bawn by Henry J Byron, London (undated). 'Henry James Byron's burlesque on The Colleen Bawn, was first produced at Drury-lane Theatre in 1861' (*The Era*, 19 April 1884 & 3 July 1897).

1861
The Bride of Garryowen, or The Colleen Bawn, drama in two acts by Henry Young, licensed for performance at Theatre Royal, Wolverhampton.

1861
The Very latest edition of the Cooleen drawn from a novel source, or, The Great Sensation Diving Belle, burlesque in one act by Martin Dutnall and J B Johnstone licensed for performance at the Surrey.

1861
Miss Eily O'Connor, burlesque in one act by H R Byron, licensed for performance at the Theatre Royal, Drury Lane.

1862
The Lily of Killarney, an opera by Sir Jules Benedict was based on the story of the Colleen Bawn (from which opera silent films versions were made).

1862
The Colleen Bawn Settled At Last, farce in one act by W Brough and A Halliday, licensed for performance at the Lyceum.

1862
Kathleen Mavourneen; or, St Patrick's Eve, drama in three acts by William Travers, licensed for performance at the Pavillion. William Travers Pope (c1824-1880), actor and dramatist: '*Kathleen Mavourneen*, a production which we cannot speak of in high terms, as the language in it is very poor … the entire construction of the play is a wretchedly bad copy of *The Colleen Bawn* and *Peep o'Day* combined' (*The Era*, 27 November 1864). '[Theatre Royal, Scarborough] The principal attraction has been the great Irish sensational drama entitled *Kathleen Mavourneen; or, St Patrick's Eve*, written and produced by the present manager, Mr William Travers' (*The Era,* 24 March 1867). 'Mr William Pope, better known as William Travers, died on August 31st after a long illness aged 54. He was the author *of Kathleen Mavourneen, The Watercress Girl, Temptation* and scores of other successful dramas' (*Lloyds Weekly*, 12 Sept 1880).

1862
Recollections of an Irish Police Magistrate and Other Reminiscences of the South of Ireland by Henry Robert Addison, London 1862, 'The Colleen Bawn', pp142-154.

1868
Ellen Hanly, or a True History of The Colleen Bawn by Rev Richard Fitzgerald, MA, *who knew her in life and saw her in death*, Moffat, Dublin, 1868.

1953

Death Sails the Shannon: The Tragic [Authentic] Story of the Colleen Bawn the facts and the fiction by William MacLysaght and Sigerson Clifford, Kerryman, Tralee, 1953.

Appendix 2

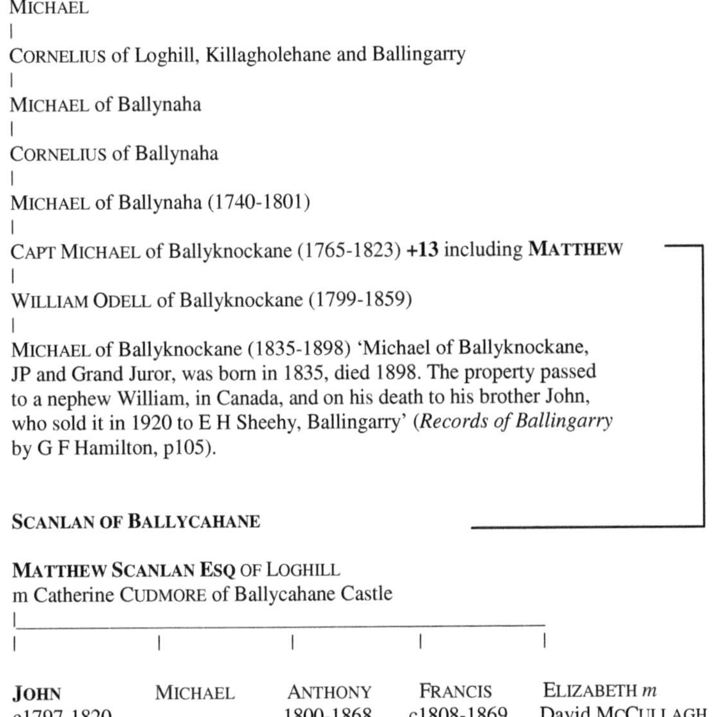

SCANLAN OF BALLYNAHA & BALLYKNOCKANE

MICHAEL
|
CORNELIUS of Loghill, Killagholehane and Ballingarry
|
MICHAEL of Ballynaha
|
CORNELIUS of Ballynaha
|
MICHAEL of Ballynaha (1740-1801)
|
CAPT MICHAEL of Ballyknockane (1765-1823) **+13** including **MATTHEW**
|
WILLIAM ODELL of Ballyknockane (1799-1859)
|
MICHAEL of Ballyknockane (1835-1898) 'Michael of Ballyknockane, JP and Grand Juror, was born in 1835, died 1898. The property passed to a nephew William, in Canada, and on his death to his brother John, who sold it in 1920 to E H Sheehy, Ballingarry' (*Records of Ballingarry* by G F Hamilton, p105).

SCANLAN OF BALLYCAHANE

MATTHEW SCANLAN ESQ OF LOGHILL
m Catherine CUDMORE of Ballycahane Castle

JOHN	MICHAEL	ANTHONY	FRANCIS	ELIZABETH *m*
c1797-1820		1800-1868	c1808-1869	David MCCULLAGH
Hanged 1820				Died 1831

Note spelling variations:
Ballynaha: Ballinaha, Ballynahagh, Ballynahaha, Ballinahaha, Ballinaher
Ballyknockane: Ballinokane, Ballynockane
Loghill: Loughill
Ballycahane: Ballycathan, Ballycahan, Ballicane, Ballycahaan, Ballichahane

Appendix 3: Research Correspondence

21 February 2011 22:05:57
Hi Eileen
Queen Victoria loved the play the Colleen Bawn, which opened at the Adelphi in Sept 1860, and there's a good history attached to the queen's favourite play. The story behind it all interests me the most. Boucicault's play was based on a book by Gerald Griffin called The Collegians, based on a murder and subsequent trial in Limerick in the early nineteenth century. What has always troubled me is why Boucicault set the play in Killarney, and not the banks of the Shannon, where the murder occurred. The story runs thus: an Ellen Hanley (two spellings as always) went missing near Glin in Co Limerick in 1819, and a body was later washed up on the banks of the Shannon, identified by a beach jury, and two men were later arrested, sent for trial and both hanged in March and July 1820, maybe there's something in the press which might give key to the Killarney connection? Daniel O'Connell the liberator defended the accused, John Scanlan, the other man involved was Stephen Sullivan, Scanlan's boatman. The Kerry link might come from Sullivan. It may be that the Dublin born Boucicault spent time in Killarney and knew it well enough to transfer all the ugly scenes from Limerick to this town, and transform what was a brutal murder into something artistic. Or it may be there is more of Kerry in this story than apparent.

02 November 2011 17:48:40
Hi Eileen
I really enjoyed the Colleen Bawn article, did you note how they were sailing across from Tarbert? I would actually like to know more about John Scanlan, so much has been written about Ellen Hanley. Maybe it's time for a reappraisal of the story.

02 November 2011 21:05:52
Hi Jan
I think a new Colleen Bawn story is called for and why was not Scanlon's execution published as was Sullivan's? The only thing I found said that the other person (Scanlon) was executed the previous month and was from a well known family in Limerick. More money talking?

02 November 2011 21:46:24
Hi Eileen
Your Colleen Bawn article has given me a lovely evening's distraction, slumped on the sofa and searching the web and newspaper archive. Very odd that you should observe the lack of reportage of Scanlan's execution, it

seems he was so powerfully connected that his case was successfully kept out of the press. Anyway, not being put off by so minor a thing, I've ploughed on and was just about to shut down when I noted in a 1960s review of the Colleen a comment that added a new name: Fitzgibbon. Further on in another 1960s article I read he was of Ballycahane House, Croom, Co Limerick. And so he is, I googled this and found his name attached to the place.

03 November 2011 20:53:51
Hello Jan
Being bored I looked elsewhere. Scanlan intrigues me. How on earth was the murder initially kept quiet when so many more comparatively minor offences were reported? I'm enclosing what I found (for a rainy day). Glad you found an address. In 1822 a party of some 300 people stormed and burned down Ballycahane House (after removing the horses from the stables) but doesn't give the name of the inhabitants merely stating it was unoccupied at the time. Again almost as if it was forbidden to mention a name. Other bdms could give some possible connections. One day Janet you must resurrect this story. Now early night for me. I have to be at the Dorothy Hyman Sports Centre by 9a.m. endeavouring to get fit enough to participate fully in Hayley's troop:):)

05 November 2011 16:25:20
Hi Eileen
After reading the Scanlon docs, I think like you it's a job that should be done, maybe you can put it on your long list of things to do to gather whatever is available, inc Sullivan's case as that may hold a few clues about Scanlan, and I can then add it to my long list of things to do☺ Isn't it incredible how the Scanlans managed to keep it completely out of the press, what was the name of that rebel newspaper during the Queen research which printed everything? Was it Reynolds? Can't even say if and where he was buried. Often at those times the bodies were given for dissection. I noticed reading through the churches this morning that Rev Jebb had his father's (the judge) notes on the murder case, imagine getting hold of those! I looked up George Leake, whose name is mentioned in the burning report, he was son of W F Leake, and built a residence Rathkeale Abbey, perhaps the principal landholder at the time.

14 January 2012 17:52:50
Hi Eileen
I read the new Colleen Bawn material I sourced yesterday. It was another of those 'true histories' written by the grandson of Judge Jebb, Heneage M Jebb, from papers inherited (remember I made a note about getting my

hands on them somewhere earlier?). Anyway, a few extra facts thrown in, like Scanlan was arrested by Gerald Blennerhassett, JP of Riddlestown (how aptly named) and that so confident were Scanlan's friends that he wouldn't go down for it that a Captain Osborne sent his carriage to the courthouse to collect Scanlan and had organized a dinner party at his house for him that evening. Another very appropriate comment was that Rev Henry Gubbins attended him at the scaffold. Gubbins later said that Scanlan had suffered for a crime he had not committed. I wonder why Scanlan was hanged?

05 February 2012 12:54:10
Hi Eileen
I've been having a lazy trawl on the internet this morning, and had a look at the newspaper site for the Aileen Moriarty murder discovery at Inch in 1905, the murder supposedly taking place 50 years earlier. Oddly enough, I found an 1844 murder at Glannaheera (Glennahira), near Inch, of Maurice Wallace, caretaker to Mr W Burke of Castlemaine, by Ignatius Moriarty who had been ejected from a farm there. He was attempting to flee by boat to Ipswich when arrested. The Inquest held by Justin Supple. I dug a little more and Wallace may have been a bible reader at one point at Achill. It all seems so familiar. Don't know anymore about the body unearthed in 1905 though, but the romanticisation, the Spanish lover, etc I take with a pinch of salt. I have a sort of idea forming about The Poor Man's Daughter (Scanlan murder/Colleen Bawn) reproduced with notes and intro etc to incorporate murders like the one above and also the 'Sailor' story I have (one of Froude's, also about the romanticisation of a murder) and fit them all under one 'book' roof. I'd like to strip the stories back to the fact, and leave it at that.

05 February 2012 17:25:29
Hello Jan
I love idea of Killings and Keenings in Kerry :) I've been looking again at Sullivan and Scanlan - the latter being as elusive as Bartram. Its cold, cold cold over here but at least the snow has melted away today. I hope the weather improves before your trip to England.

28 March 2012 21:09:22
Hi Eileen
I seem to have wasted most of the last hours on Massy, trying fruitlessly to determine genealogy of Rev Godfrey. I think the Massys could be the Limerick version of the Herberts. I tried to follow the line of Stagdale, as the booklet specifically says third son of Hugh Massy Esq of Stagdale, but this led to Williams and Johns and to cut a long story short, I've just put it

all away. What I did notice though, were a few Scanlans, an Hon George Massy of Stagdale married Miss Scanlan of Ballynaha in 1792, and I noted among the jury members of a libel case in 1816 William Massy of Stagdale and Michael Scanlan. Worth making a note of for future ref. Remember Colleen Bawn Scanlan was of a substantial landed family.

02 April 2012 11:39:47
Hi Eileen
Your Scanlan doc sent all my plans out of the window, as I went back to the Massy family tree, and think I've added a few more pieces. I suspect - with special emphasis on suspect - our Godfrey Massy may have descended from the branch of Rev Godfrey Massy of Mount Sion, Co Limerick, who was vicar Dysert, Limerick and Prebend of Limerick. He was son of Col Hugh Massy, and his eldest brother was 1st Lord Massy, another brother was Archdeacon Massy of Ardfert. I looked him up, he was also rector of Kilcornan Limerick 1736-82, married Jane Purdon but died without issue. This Godfrey of Mount Sion had a second son, Rev William Massy, who built Glenwilliam, Limerick in 1797. So just making a note of it all as I go along, because Rev William is bound to turn up, they will all come together at some point.

28 May 2012 12:45:40
Hi Eileen
Many thanks for Ballingarry, what a trove. I found another account of the Ellen Scanlan (Colleen Bawn) case, not exactly contemporary, about 50 years after the event, but it did have a transcript of the depositions taken at the time and in that I found that John Scanlan was son of William Scanlan Esq, of Ballycahane. It was amusing to read the biased text of the 1866 author, who had Scanlan, from the distance of 50 years, tried and sentenced in one paragraph as an utterly evil rogue.

28 May 2012 15:36:26
Hi Eileen
Just been looking through list of Scanlan deaths on Limerick website and wonder, could below be Scanlan's father? I found that he was JP in Limerick in 1829, and Lewis in 1830s had W Scanlan Esq of Ballino Kane, or Ballinokane I also found. I think this might have been Ballyknockane (or Ballynockane as I've also found) House, a Scanlan property in Ballingarry. I found a number of the family at this address, the death of a Frances Margaret Scanlan of Ballyknockane in Nov 1868 aged 90, if she was William's sister then it could have been him who died in 1859 (below). John Scanlan was about 20-23 when he was executed in 1820 so this could be his

father: Scanlan, William, Ballynockane, 09/07/1859, served as High Sheriff of Co. Limerick; d. at Rathmines, Dublin.

29 May 2012 16:30:32
Hi Jan
Now I would like to differ with you re Scanlan's father and put forward another suggestion. The True Story of Colleen Bawn published c.1862 says that Scanlan's father died during John's infancy So let's say around 1795-1800. John Scanlan (Colleen Bawn) it is also said, was a former Lieutenant. I found a John Scanlan promoted to Lieutenant in 1797. In 1800 a John Scanlan was murdered in the Limerick/Kerry border area. He was obviously of some importance as the reports seem to assume that readers would know of the man. Unfortunately there is no more mention of the murder other than the enclosed. John Scanlan Colleen Bawn would have been around 3 or 4 at this time. So was this John Scanlan the father of John Scanlan (Colleen Bawn) ? John grows up to follow in his father's career? Another interesting find was the death notice of a Rebekah Eliza Massey, relict of a John Scanlan d. 1863 age of 70 - right age for Scanlan's sister and the name Massey sort of keeps it in the big family pot? Second file is a list of Scanlan bdms for you. Very small gene pool☺ Just a few bits of Ballingarry left so please send more. And just maybe another novel in the Colleen Bawn story. I recall reading the description of the horses refusing to pull the cart with John Scanlan over the bridge. Was he hanged or spirited away. It's just that I find it difficult to believe after reading commutations of sentences for people of the lower order that Justice Jebb would refuse an appeal? Maybe one day a tale of a 'Speed Bonny boat over the seas to Australia' and then years later he returns in disguise and inherits his rights.

30 May 2012 10:58:04
Hi Eileen
I LOVE your conspiracy theory that he was spirited away overseas, much like Elvis and Diana and all the others:) If we take Froude's advice, that the water at the source is the purest, then the transcript I found at the weekend is about as close as it gets. And in that transcript, it stated that Scanlan was son of William Scanlan Esq of Ballycahane. What I need to do next is check the map to see if this could possibly have been misconstrued, and was in fact Ballyknockane. If I can find no grand mansions at Ballycahane, it is a possibility. The gem you found is Rev T R Scanlan, rector of Ardglass (Down) who was son of late William Scanlan JP of Ballyknockane, grandson of Lord of the Treasury. Now we really are talking high connections. Could William JP have been a brother, perhaps eldest son of Lt William Scanlan?

30 May 2012 13:09:15
Hi Eileen
Not quite sure how I found this doc, but it certainly makes sobering reading. I'm not sure we can unravel this mystery after all ... if you have a look at the comment at the bottom of p80 and then at p72, perhaps the Michael of Ballynakill referred to, you'll see what I mean. What is interesting though is the Massy connection.

30 May 2012 19:49:30
Hello again
Help - you are confusing me. Footnote p.80 says "This Michael appears to be the Michael Scanlan who was convicted of the murder of the Colleen Bawn". But it was a JOHN Scanlan who was convicted. Purest water is nearest the source? See extracts from Stephen Sullivan's trial 1820. Different witnesses refer to him as either J. Scanlan, or Mr John. Reading the trial it seems only minimal details were deliberately published.

30 May 2012 20:05:50
Hi Eileen
First thing I spotted was the Michael/John discrepancy, even with the high people in high places, I doubt very much his name would be fabricated in the legal docs. The compilers of this new doc seem to have been descendants, my feeling is that they simply plucked Michael from 'John and Michael' in error, and clearly knew little of the case. And I think their guess was wrong, and that Matthew Scanlan and his wife Catherine were not the parents of our John, because the transcript of the trial, dated 1819, states unequivocally, 'John Scanlan, son of William Scanlan Esq of Ballycahane'. That said, I did find online today a Matthew Scanlan and John Scanlan, both listed as freemen of Limerick in 1819, perhaps Mathew (spelt two ways) was John's brother?

30 May 2012 20:17:56
Hi Jan
Forgot to add, did you notice the Liverpool Mercury bit 1869 re a male Scanlan dropping dead in street in Limerick age around 70 and said to be brother of the Scanlan hanged for murder? Now here is the challenge - find the death of a male Scanlan in Limerick between Jan/May 1869. Mystery solved! Reports said he was a well dressed man so some record should be around. Then we write the true story. OMG we could be billionaires with a Hollywood blockbuster☺

30 May 2012 20:30:05
Dear Eileen

Can you believe that you found that doc long ago, and that it has been at the back of my mind all along, niggling away, and I was only looking at it at the weekend, wondering how I could find out more. Death records from Limerick area, first thing on my list of things to do tomorrow. I just had a quick scour around, and found that the genealogy doc seems to come from The Irish Ancestor of 1972. Its founder, Rosemary ffolliott, died recently, was living for a time at Fethard, Co Tipperary, and the Midlands, she sounded a very clever - and rather nice - lady indeed if you fancy having a read.

12 June 2012 13:19:48
Hi Eileen
A delightful man at the Limerick records office has just mailed me this: Francis Scanlan, R.I.P. 02/05/1869 at North Strand, aged last birthday 60 years. Thing is, I can't remember where we go from here☺.

12 June 2012 13:28:34
Me again Eileen
Just to add to the utter confusion, just checked Francis Scanlan online Irish papers, and a different version☹

12 June 2012 13:28:34
Hi Eileen
Just airing my up to date thoughts on Scanlan, more so we can keep a record of this game of cluedo. We now have two reports, one stating Francis was a brother of John, the other stating a nephew. On the face of it, it seems more likely he was a brother, judging by the dates, but not ruling anything out. I returned to the genealogy doc and this, 'there was a family of Scanlan resident at Ballycahane, parish of Kilcornan, Co Limerick, which may be connected to the lineage'. This led me to re-check Ballycahane, because there is a parish Ballycahane, and a townland of Ballycahane, parish of Kilcornan. Lewis recorded Cpt Scanlan at Ballycahane House, Ballycahane parish and so it seems more likely that Scanlan was of the parish, not the townland. I also found in O'Donovan's notes that the name 'Hanly' was prevalent in 'Ballycahaan Upper' (with two 'a's) – the parish. Also found ref to a Ballycahan (no 'e') Castle, Croom. Perhaps the next thing to do is to plot Ballycahane House and physically go there. I haven't really got any further, and am no longer sure what I'm looking for☹. Also on rootschat: Looking for information on William MONCKTON, my 2nd great grandfather. He was born in 1824 in Amogan, Croagh, Co. Limerick and married Margaret Walsh who was born in 1829. Most of the Moncktons hailed from Ballingarry and I recall my late mother mentioning some

connection with the "Colleen Bawn" murderer, Scanlan of Ballycahane House.

12 June 2012 17:17:11
Hello Jan
Rootschat - could the connection be Ellen Walsh - the one who gave evidence at Sullivan's trial?

13 June 2012 13:18:34
Dear Eileen
Well spotted. I've been on Scanlan's case all morning, found a ref to another article that had appeared in 'The New Monthly'. The title was all I had to go on, but as you say, tenacity pays, and good old archive.org has not let me down. I found it in the American edition of the journal, and also found an edited version of the same thing by the same author in his memoirs published in 1854. It's quite sad, especially the final description of Scanlan's walk to the gallows, the scene almost Christ-like. Of course this has told me nothing more of Scanlan's parentage, but I found it interesting to read yesterday in the death of Francis Scanlon that he was the last surviving member of this particular branch, I wonder does this explain why little if anything seems to have been published in Scanlan's favour in the intervening years? Next plan to visit to Ballycahane. I checked on the map last night and firstly ruled out Kilcornan, not much in the townland of Ballycahane, and then plotted Ballycahane House. I might be able to find a few clues in the churchyard.

13 June 2012 17:21:17
Hello Jan
Searching Money Point I came up with a piece I hadn't found before. No names, only that body found. I believe this is the first (and only) mention of the case in Sept 1819. I decided to look at Majors Warburton and Ogle - they were the ones who went to Money Point when the find was reported. Do I have a suspicious mind but why would the Chief Magistrate of Police and another high ranking officer go to investigate the find of a partly decomposed naked woman's body? Murders were commonplace and the lower ranks did not receive the same police attention. Were they anticipating that a body may come to light? Then, through Warburton, I came across the story of Judith Lynchy. Jan, there are just far too many similarities with these two poor girls. I won't list them - you will see. My theory is that, hot on the heels of Judith Lynchy (Aug 1819), people in high places were smarting and could not afford more scandal. So maybe John Scanlan had to hang in an attempt to put a lid on things. I was surprised at the scant coverage of Judith Lynchy - obviously attempts were made to

keep it quiet but 'The Friend of the Oppressed' helped! Enjoy - I think you should do a completely new book on Judith Lynchy and Ellen Hanley. Just two poor girls used then disposed of ☹

14 June 2012 13:26:24
Hi Eileen
I think you've opened up a can of worms on this, and it makes me wonder how many young girls are lying in the waters of the Shannon. It gives a new dimension to Scanlan's hanging, which has never made sense, there was never a motive. I found another associated doc to your one, interesting that an O'Connell involved. The girl must have been taken in Aug 1818 and was evidently returned at the government's expense. Seems odd enough. I wonder what happened to her Eileen, whose body was it washed up in 1819? And strange no teeth in the corpse's head for identification.

14 June 2012 14:59:35
Hi Eileen
If William Borough (Burrough) Esq was convicted in 1819, he doesn't seem to have suffered too much as I found Clare related docs of his and Randal (Randall) Borough Esqs' involvement in evictions c1828-31, if the same man. I know from studying Froude that smuggling was almost unchecked at this period, I wonder did the government make a very public display of returning this girl and convicting the magistrate to shield what was going on.

14 June 2012 21:34:41
Hello Jan
I want to borrow the Dr Who tardis. Just for a few days please. I'm convinced there is an untold story behind Judith Linchy and Ellen Hanly. So where did I get today with my time travel? I debated whether somehow Judith Lynchy and Ellen Hanly could be the same dead body. No - National Archives have a file of papers relating to complaints made against Major George Warburton including a petition from Judith Lynchy (Jan-Feb 1821) to Lord Lieutenant that the £20 relief ordered by the government to be paid to her had not been paid. Warburton describes allegations made against him by Judith as "a most abominable falsehood" and said that the £20 was paid on 1 Feb 1821. I also saw a note requesting an annuity granted by the government for the support of the children of a John Macgrath 1821. (Co-defendant with William Burough) The only trace maybe is a John Macgrath going to the East India Company. Lenient sentences I think you will agree. But the timing of Judith and Ellen bugs me. Ellen 'found washed ashore' Sept 1819 - The Knight of Glin, Major Warburton and Major Ogle go out yet only The Knight of Glin gives evidence at Sullivan's trial. Warburton

was Chief of Police so if the event was important enough for him to go out then surely he would be the one to give evidence? Ellen Walsh said in evidence that when she asked Sullivan the whereabouts of 'Mrs Scanlan' he replied 'She was shipped off with the captain of a ship". Sound familiar? So both the girls were: Around in the same locality during the same couple of years/"Shipped off with the captain of a ship"/Had competition from wealthier young jealous women/Would appear to be similar age/Appear to be from poor families/Flattered maybe by attention of a young 'gent'/Had no one to speak up for them/No mother mentioned for Judith and Ellen brought up by grandfather/Buroughs ex military Scanlan and Sullivan too. The more I read the more it is like the awful grooming of young girls that is prevalent today. I'm enclosing a late piece 1888, a journalist talking to a Michael O'Connell (descendant of The Friend of the Oppressed?) I don't know if you already have the full piece but here it is. Also a couple of bits on Shannakyle Churchyard - Ellen's grave. Lots and lots to try and work out - Jephson, the Pro Collector - was he the son of the Archdeacon of Cork or was he of Anne Jephson, mother of Roger Casement? How long have you got? Oh and yes - the date given for the death of William Burough Aussie paper is out by 2 years. Clare Journal 2 Dec 1852 says "Last Monday, at Querin House, Ret. Commander William Burough, an officer, who in earlier life had much service" please write the book!
PS: Forgot to make my point, the Lord Lieutenant, having just got Major Warburton (the first ever appointed Chief of Police) out of one big mess wasn't prepared to get him out of another by reprieving Scanlan.

15 June 2012 10:57:17
Hi Eileen
Scanlan: like you he has my head done in! I spent hours last night poring over documents and tying myself up in knots, but I have reached the same conclusion as you. I think it's Columbo we need on this one. As far as Scanlan goes, I concluded during my late evening walk in the rain that there are so many discrepancies with names and dates that these alone are sufficient to show a miscarriage of justice. Not even the alleged victim's name is correct, you might have noticed in the 1825 account the other day it was either Hanly/ey or Hanlon, same with the witness name, Walsh and Welsh. The dates are worse: absconded end of June, murdered 4th July (as per her headstone online) but seen in company of Scanlan and Sullivan 13 and 14 July. Body washed up 'latter end of July', interred on the beach, inquest in September. Why so long? Again various dates: Sept 10th, 19th etc. I dread to think of the condition of the body by that stage. The doc you sent yesterday about Money Point stated Major Ogle attended; the court doc I have documenting the inquest states it was held by John F Fitzgerald, Knight of Glin, George Warburton and Thomas Odell at which the

following was concluded: ‘we find on a view of the body buried on the shore at Carndotta that the woman exposed to our view was murdered. We find that such murder was effected by strangling the body with the rope found about her neck. We find that such murder was committed by John Scanlan or Stephen Sullivan or by both’. This was before the trial! Easy in those days, wasn’t it! I noticed that most of the witnesses to this inquest-cum-trial left their mark, ‘x’. But I also wonder about so many other things: the uncle whose money was taken; I would view him as a prime suspect (and he was a ropemaker). He would have had a great motive for wanting his cash back. The stolen sum was a lot of money in those days. I think the powers-that-be wanted the case closed fast; and your find yesterday explains why. There’s the motive! It has cast a wholly different light on the story with the revelation by ‘the friend of the oppressed’ in human trafficking. It may simply be a complete coincidence that the Colleen Bawn was murdered and drew unwanted attention on the port of Slattery. It is a replica of Froude’s tale of the sailor. Question: Why did the government go to the expense of returning Judith Lynchy (Lynch?) to Ireland. This is the question I keep asking myself. Did the woman with the powerful connections overstep her mark? How could a poor woman have commanded such an act? Was it that the government wanted to be seen to be doing ‘the right thing’. There are documents from the trial of Scanlan at the national library; I’d be more interested in reading those you’ve found related to Judith. Thanks for the Borough date. When I read the document again last night, I noticed that he was Cpt William Borough who in 1815 was employed in the preventive service on the west coast. Could he have also been an Esq? Or could he have become one, if he came in from the sea☺ Could the captain and the magistrate be the same?

15 June 2012 15:58:17
Hello Jan
I managed to download this from the NA. Enjoy.

16 June 2012 19:09:54
Hi Eileen
I have absolutely no idea how you managed to download that document. I don't know how you read it, but I read it - from the final paragraph - as authored by whoever was at the helm of the Limerick Chronicle? And yet the letter (or the one very similar) published in the paper gave the impression of distance, 'I reside remote from the scene of tyranny'. Hmm. I think not. I've had a quick look at Homes and O'Brien; O'Brien estates in Limerick vast, ie, Dromoland, will have to look on map to see what is where, Homes I had no luck with but plenty of well-heeled Holmes, inter-marrying with the ones now so familiar to us. I particularly liked the fact

that of Borough it states 'this man is a justice of the peace, and a lieut of the Royal Navy'. There's so much in it I'll have to read it again. I drove to Limerick yesterday evening, and Ballycahane church. As if anything is ever straightforward, I thought I'd be able to jot down a few dates and have Scanlan genealogy solved. Not to be of course, there are very few graves to be found there, two of the oldest looking were covered in ivy which when removed, were illegible. Just one tomb and it was covered in ivy, a few headstones to O'Neills and Leonard, and that was it. Nearby Ballycahane House (church would have been almost in the back yard) was knocked in the 1970s and a farm there now, just a small ruin of Ballycahane Castle. Even the coat of arms on the church wall was faded beyond recognition. This morning I tried a different angle and sought to track down parish records; the RCB now has a very handy up-to-date list of the records it holds but Ballycahane not included. So where to next with Scanlan? I had spotted a couple of Scanlan headstones in Kilpeacon churchyard and through them, goodness knows how at this stage, I somehow found a note on a genealogy website that stated a Cudmore owned Ballycahane Castle connected to the Colleen Bawn. I searched on and found ref to a John Cudmore and Catherine Dalton who had Alice Cudmore who married c1797 Richard Smyth jr. Also found a Dalton death in 1797 at Ballycahane Castle of 'Miss DALTON, a maiden lady, daughter of the late Michael DALTON, of Ballycahane, County of Limerick, Esq'. So a new name to go on? Perhaps Alice Cudmore had a sister who married a Scanlan, the dates would fit well don't you think, if the sister married at about the same time, as John Scanlan was born c1797?

17 June 2012 11:19:47
Dear Eileen
It's always good to think! Walking Roxie last night it occurred to me that when John Scanlan was born, the church wasn't built. Nearest church Kilpeacon, where baptism records do exist, but only from 1893. One step forward, one step back ... So I went back over our old mails, and that gem, Fitzgibbon. I went back to the genealogy document, and on p79, this: 'Matthew Lane Scanlan of Duckstown and later of Ballylin, will proved 1803, married at Croagh Jan 1773 Elizabeth Fitzgibbon. By deed dated 9 Oct 1777 they agreed to separate and live asunder because of controversies, disputes and disagreements for some time past and £113 was settled on Elizabeth and their 2 sons, who were committed to her care by the separation settlement of which Gibbon Fitzgibbon of Ballysheeda Co Limerick was trustee. She died 17 May 1813 having had issue John and Thomas.' The date wouldn't fit for it to be her son. He would have to have been born before the separation in 1777. Did John have a John, nothing more is given of him in the genealogy doc, but the other son Thomas, born

1776 buried 20 Aug 1822 aged 46 married Bridget daughter of Philip Nunan of Moyge Liscarroll Co Cork. She died June 1817 having had an issue of 8, inc a son John, born 1814, who married at Walcot, near Bath, on 4 May 1840 as 'John Fitzgibbon Scanlan Esq' of Limerick son of Michael (sic) to Rebekah Elizabeth Massey etc. I googled John Fitzgibbon Scanlan and a book, Officers of the Royal Marines on Reserved Half-Pay, lists JFS as a First Lieutenant on reserved half pay in September 1814. But so many questions: where were he and his sisters raised, if he was in the custody of his mother? Did John Fitzgibbon Scanlan, who would have been born between late 1773 to 1775, marry (perhaps a Cudmore), have issue the First Lieutenant, and die young like his own father? Now I also found a legal doc online, Fitzgibbon vs Scanlan, a case heard in the court of chancery in 1813 (on appeal), and from it I found that Matthew Lane Scanlan did 'inter-marry' Elizabeth Fitzgibbon in 1773 and he died in 1793 leaving two sons and 2 daughters. The eldest son died unmarried without issue and his money went to his youngest son, the respondent in the case, namely JF Scanlan. The case was about land (of course) and from the judgment, it would seem that Fitzgibbon, the appelant, was also a son, as he is referred to as administrator of Matthew Lane Scanlan his late father'. I also re-read the letter about Judith. It is gossipy; was Mr Oppressed trying to get at Mr O'Brien via the actions of his wife, or trying to get at Borough? Was Borough, in his new anti-smuggling capacity, in the way? Was he set up by O'Brien? Smuggling is at the heart of this.

17 June 2012 19:07:59
Hi Eileen
Can't help thinking we're closing in on Scanlan. Been going through your docs yet again, and your John Scanlan doc from the Glasgow Herald of 1862 stated 'He lost his father in his infancy ... when he grew up he entered the army and attained the rank of lieutenant. This more or less fits in with the official marine doc, which listed him half-pay 1814, and also I found him on another navy list under the Royal Marine Forces as first lieutenant on reserved half-pay on 1 May 1812. He may have been based in Dublin, from where he had returned with Sullivan.

17 June 2012 21:23:23
Hello Jan
A selection for you - yes I agree we are slowly moving in. Just don't hope we come to a dead end. Cudmore, Mathew Lane Scanlan and the piece I liked most John Fitzgibbon. Even if it doesn't fit, it is a great piece. As it is Sunday then a little scandal with Hannah Villiers. Yes I know she is not one of yours but I liked it. So for the time being I think I will just continue to

trawl with a large mesh - who knows what may come up.

18 June 2012 13:12:12
Good day Eileen
My head is spinning from Scanlans and Gibbons. From official docs, we know that Mathew Lane Scanlan married Elizabeth Fitzgibbon in 1773 (who died 1813). From the legal doc of 1813 we know they had two sons and two daughters. The genealogy doc gives the sons' names as John and Thomas. So far so good. So I've been following these facts as closely as I can. I started by looking for clues on Elizabeth Fitzgibbon, and found that the Fitzgibbons were Earls of Clare. The court doc stated that Elizabeth had property on her marriage under her father's will, his name given as Thomas. Fortunately, the Earls of Clare were short lived, and from Debrett's, I found that Thomas Fitzgibbon (1708-1780) of Ballyseeda (or Ballysheedy) Co Limerick had four boys: John, Patrick, Thomas, and Gibbon. The eldest John was of Mountshannon, Co Limerick and was father of the first Earl of Clare (John, 1792-1851). The genealogy of John is given but what I suspect from the dates is that Elizabeth might possibly have been the daughter of the third son, Thomas, whose time-line is similar to that of his brother. And so, this would have been a noble and powerful connection. Moved onto Mathew Lane Scanlan, peerage has another by this name and I found others, but the one most interesting is the one at national archives of 1818, which also ties quite nicely with the rebel doc you found. Could this be Thomas 'Fitzgibbon' Scanlan? Perhaps one brother might help lead to the other? 'CSO/RP/1818/579 Petition of Thomas Scanlan, Brooklodge, Rathkeale, County Limerick, to Earl Talbot, Lord Lieutenant, Dublin Castle, requesting a post of employment. Refers to military service and reduction due to 'unavoidable fatalities' and mentions responsibilities for a family of ten children; states his father Mathew Lane Scanlan served as Justice of the Peace in County Limerick 'at a time when it was greatly disturbed by Bands of Rebels' and that through 'his personal and unceasing exertions at the head of the Military completely Subdued them and restored the County to a State of perfect quiet and security'.

18 June 2012 19:21:58
Hello Jan
Here are more for you to sift and pound. If I came across the correct surname and roughly correct district then I saved it. You just never know. Not sure if Burke's Peerage is in agreement with me on some things. Hayes Scanlan interests me. I couldn't find anything on the Hayes v Hayes' Scanlan estate case. I need now to sit and try and absorb my day's finds. I'm not sure if you have The Times coverage of Sullivan trial - bin it if you have. I just noticed a few differences.

19 June 2012 10:52:38
Hi Eileen
I liked the Thomas Fitzgibbon port collector, ties in quite nicely with Judith. Slotting your dates in the Scanlan family tree, coming together quite nicely, except our John. That said, I went back to drawing board earlier and started wondering, was there another Fitzgibbon girl married a Scanlan perhaps? So much is wrong. I found another Scanlan pedigree, there is a Francis in the family tree, and the lack of this name has been worrying me a lot. Also a footnote speaks of a connection to Lord Clare. Not sure what any of this is telling me yet, but it does give new leads.

19 June 2012 13:12:47
Me again Eileen
I've been trying to establish birth dates for the 7 boys and 7 girls of Michael Scanlan; found in a book on Cox genealogy = William Cox, Esq (born 1765) married in 1796, Mary, daughter of Michael Scanlon, County Limerick. This would make Mary born c1770s, and I calculate Michael's offspring would have been born c1760s to 1770s. Another of the children, Elizabeth, her marriage to Hon George Eyre Massy was I think in 1791 which would tally. John Fitzgibbon Scanlan, it states, married a Wheeler cousin at Bath (note in the footnote his father was related to General Sir Hugh Wheeler). It seems likely he would have married in the 1790s as with his sisters? Could he have been Scanlan's father? There does seem to be a Wheeler connection. The older genealogy doc I found stated, 'John (son of Mathew Lane Scanlon) born 1814 married at Walcot, Bath, 4 May 1840 as 'John Fitzgibbon Scanlan' of Limerick, son of Michael Scanlan Esq (*sic*) to Rebekah Elizabeth Massy, daughter of Hugh Wheeler'. The compiler assumed the 'son of' bit was an error. The names are sufficiently noble to help conceal Scanlan's identity for 200 years.

19 June 2012 15:34:03
Hi Eileen
Just wondering is it a case of back to the drawing board. Just found an article by Kerry historian Mary Agnes Hickson, in which she states the parents of John Scanlon and Stephen Sullivan 'were still living' in 1829. She further states, 'the junior branch of the Scanlan family of Limerick county, to which the unhappy youth belonged, is long extinct, and the statement that he ever was the heir of the owners of Ballynaha and Ballyknockane, high sheriffs of Limerick county in 1796 and 1826, is one of many falsehoods'. Groan. I now wonder if the Cpt Scanlan of Ballycahane mentioned in Lewis's Topographical of 1830s was his father, I wonder was it Cpt William Scanlan of Ballycahane?
What do you think?

19 June 2012 22:08:01
Hello Jan
What do I think? I'll tell you tomorrow when my poor tired brain has tried to make sense of all this new info. My knee jerk reaction is that Mary Hickson is not correct as there had to be someone of influence to gag the press but ... A beautiful summer day today - little light gardening. I saw a gardener doing some work next door and asked him if he would shape down a conifer for me before it got out of hand. Poor man - he had to balance on some step ladders whilst holding a lethal long hedge cutter. When he finished he said that he was leaving me the trimmings as a gift. Ok I said - how much? "I'm not charging you anything providing you never ask me to do it again" he replied! By the way how did we get back to Scanlan?

20 June 2012 10:09:17
Dear Eileen
How did we get to Scanlan? Can't remember, but we've been on his case for some time on and off. I am aware that Mary Agnes Hickson's work was thorough and honest. Russell is an admirer, and is working on another edition of her Kerry history books, taken from the press, if I remember correctly. If I was a gambling girl, I'd put my money on her. Her statement about the parents being alive and the allusion to Ballinaha gives it away. She drew on Tennyson's The Princess to make her point. That Scanlan's parents were alive makes a lot more sense in many ways. It would have been a heavy trial for them in those days, and the protection they were given by their supporters must have been most needed. The execution was unjust, but there were a lot of injustices in those times, as we've learned. Stories grow legs here - rapidly - but as you know there is often an element of truth running through them. The story of Scanlan being a military man points my attention to John Fitzgibbon Scanlan, captain of marines. Father and son in the military seems plausible. I suspect he married a Dalton/Cudmore, I think I read a Catherine on rootsweb, must check, and that is how he came to be associated with Ballycahane. He is the only captain in the family tree (incidentally, somewhere in the later generations I saw that someone had named their child Colleen). Lewis identified a Cpt Scanlan in the 1830s at Ballycahane House, and by the 40s, it's the residence of Rev S Connery, p.p. I wonder also if Cpt Scanlan remarried late in life, as was the way then, and is actually the Cpt Scanlan who married at Bath in 1840? No wonder the other compilers got confused if this is the case. He died there too, but was 'of Limerick' in the death notice of the Kerry Evening Post in 1844. There were two daughters (sisters) too mentioned in the court statements, one at Kilkee, one at Ballycahane, who is to say there was not a son Francis too? Your William Scanlan finds I managed to slot into the tree too, in fact so many of them. I'm going to try to get a military record for Scanlan.

20 June 2012 12:08:14
Hi Eileen
Just for the record, I found a notice that a Michael Scanlan Esq died 'last Tuesday at Ballynakill Co Limerick' (Limerick Chronicle, 8/8/1782). Been wondering about Ballynakill, and just found a note in topographical book that 'Ballynakill House was burnt by insurgents 24 Feb 1822 when it was converted into a barrack for soldiers'. May have been rebuilt, and there was another captain, Michael, who continued the line.

20 June 2012 14:58:18
Hi Eileen
Me again. Took the Scanlans right back to their Catholic roots today. While searching Ballynakill, I found that Michael Matthew Scanlan Esq, Matthew Scanlan Esq of Ballynaha, and Mrs Eliza O'Scanlan of Ballynakill subscribed to a 1770s book by Dr Laurence Nihell, later Bishop of Kilfenora, entitled Rational Self-Love. And when the bishop's brother, Dr James Nirell, died in 1759 he set to work on his brother's manuscripts in a History of the Redemption of Man which 'he means to publish as soon as the state of his health will permit him'.

20 June 2012 20:42:22
Hello Jan
Just a thought - National Library holds a letter from Daniel O'Connell to his wife Mary written March 15th 1820 re the unsuccessful defence of John Scanlan. Who paid Daniel O'Connell to defend?

21 June 2012 09:51:34
Hi Eileen
I have an extract of that letter - who employed O'Connell? Good question, and idea; the National Library holds the papers from the trial, perhaps ultimately I'll have to go to Dublin, as I'd love to do. But before that, I had another idea this morning ... I tried to find Ballinaha House on the map last night, and noticed it was spelt on both maps Ballinahaha House, and a search this morning revealed a lovely website to the Carey family of Ballingarry in which I spotted William Scanlan Esq on the Griffiths Valuation of 1850s, and also on the 1826 tithe applotment for the townland of Ballinahaha. And this has got me thinking, if I can find the Tithe applotment record for Ballycahane of 1826 …

21 June 2012 10:44:04
Hi Eileen
Do you recall in the genealogy doc it stated, 'there was a family of Scanlan resident at Ballycahane, parish of Kilcornan, Co Limerick possibly

descending from Michael of Ballynakill ... A Matthew Scanlan of Ballycahane, living 1815, with wife Catherine, had sons John and Michael. If there was a Matthew Scanlan at Ballycahane in 1815, and a Matthew Scanlan there in 1826, there is a strong possibility it could be Scanlan's father? If you follow the Michael of Ballynakill line, it gives very little. He was the third in line of the Ballinaha branch, will proved 1764. Only clue is his son Michael may have married Elizabeth Massy. I did find a death record, 'died at Ballynakill Co Limerick, Michael Scanlan Esq' in Limerick Chronicle, 8 Aug 1782. Any thoughts? I'm still inclined towards the Scanlan/Cudmore/Dalton link to Ballycahane. Did John Fitzgibbon Scanlan, captain of marines, in the parallel branch of the family, encourage this young man into the services?

21 June 2012 11:53:16
Hi Eileen
I must be driving you mad and I can't quite recall how I have obtained this information because I can't track down the source but it states this anyway: 'Catherine Cudmore, Cripps sister-in-law, was the wife of Matthew Scanlon and mother to John Scanlon. Alderman John Cripps (Senior)'. I searched Alderman Cripps and up popped a book, Select Committee Report of Limerick 1819 plus a bit in it about an Alderman Cripps in Freemen of Limerick 1760s who was involved with Limerick port. It sounds fishy (pardon the pun).

21 June 2012 12:07:30
Me again!
Just found this on a Crips of Limerick family tree (two spellings as usual): FJ 24 July 1790 'Married John Crips of Cahirnarry to Miss Cudmore, daughter of John Cudmore of Ballycahane' I noticed elsewhere in the tree there are Dalton-Crips. Is this the Crips sister-in-law, the Cudmore married to Mathew Scanlan? This seems to be adding up?

21 June 2012 12:15:19
And finally, before I drive you completely mad Eileen, those men listed as freemen of Limerick: Scanlan Mathew Esqre, Ballycahane 28/6/1819; Scanlan John Esqre, Ballycahane 28/6/1819. Father and son? John was still alive in 1819, though not so much a freeman.

21 June 2012 12:31:46
Hi Eileen
I promise to leave you in peace now for a while, but this doc I just found dated 1799 made me smile, I think we know them all! The Scanlans listed are:

Michael Scanlan, Esq; Ballynaha.
Michael Scanlan, jun. Esq; Ballinaha. (magistrate)
Mathew Scanlan, Esq; Strand-field.
Connell Scanlan, Esq; Ballynaha.
Thomas Scanlan, Esq; Gortnacrehy.

I think John Scanlan's parents were Matthew Scanlan Esq and Catherine Cudmore. All I need now is (for you☺) to prove it.

21 June 2012 15:44:04
Hi Eileen
Had a trawl around the national archives this afternoon, and came across the last will of John Fitzgibbon Scanlan. I rapidly took out my credit card and ordered. I've just had a quick read through, which is nigh on impossible with the old writing, and it will need to be painstakingly transcribed, but from my first reading, a marriage in 1840, to Rebekah Eliza Massey Scanlan (otherwise Wheeler).

21 June 2012 20:11:28
Hello Jan
What a day you have had! I've downloaded the will and will have a go at transcribing it before I attempt anything more. Meanwhile today I took the Robbie Coltrane approach. The obit for Matthew Scanlan, Sept 1867, is crying out for attention. My take on it: The terminology is unusual for that period. It seems to have been penned by someone related or very close to him - someone who knew how much suffering had been caused to Matthew and the injustices he had carried from the age of around 14 or 15 years that he would have been when John Scanlan was executed. Did the writer know that more could have been done for John Scanlan. Did the higher end of the Scanlans not do enough? The obituary reads like an apology that should have been made years before.

22 June 2012 09:50:42
Hi Eileen
Oh how I love your dry sense of humour, and the irony of Jane Scanlan rescuing a boy from drowning in the Shannon! Just looked her up, she got her RHS medal by her rescue of Vincent Kenny. Anyway Eileen, you're going to kill me! Last night I thought I should really read that 1953 Colleen book - which I bought in 2007 – properly. And so I sat down and read, it contains info on the Scanlan family, including the Cudmores (don't hit me!) and so I thought to myself, so what, I constantly reinvent the wheel, but look what I learn along the way! So new facts, new direction: 'The first recorded Scanlan in Ballycahane who by lease dated 28 Sept 1787 acquired from the Right Hon John FitzGibbon [the Earl of Clare] was Michael

Scanlan. This Michael Scanlan had a brother, Morgan Scanlan, and a son Francis Scanlan, mentioned in the lease'. This Scanlan seems to be the one in the 'main' tree Eileen, he had a brother Morgan, and a son Francis, dates fit. 'Matthew Scanlan married Catherine Cudmore of Ballycahane Castle and was the father of John Scanlan, the principal figure in the Colleen Bawn story'. Aren't we clever working that out for ourselves! I've had another look at the tree, and by putting the two existing genealogy docs together, I'm getting a better picture. There was a Matthew Scanlan, brother of Michael and John Fitzgibbon (of the will) but he is supposed to have been a military man who died 1840. That said, Lewis commented in 1830s that Cpt Scanlan was resident at Ballycahane House. Main problem now is who was Matthew, and how does he fit in. Can you search for all things Mathew/Matthew? I feel we are a step away, and yet ...Matthew Scanlan and Catherine Cudmore had John, Michael, Francis (our man in Limerick who dropped dead) Anthony, and Elizabeth, who married Dr David McCullough, MD, of Bruff. There is another sister mentioned in the court docs, but only one given in this book. Quite a bit of info on the Cudmores, and Crips. Matthew Scanlan is described as of Loughill (Loghill) Co Limerick at their marriage. There's more, but this is the essence.

22 June 2012 16:50:01
Hi Eileen
For what it's worth, I've also noted in one of the legal docs published in the book that in 1809, Mathew Scanlan Esq was of Triphall Co Limerick; in 1799, he was of Strand-field, Co Limerick. Only ref I can find to these places is for the latter, where someone used to fish by the Shannon.

22 June 2012 18:33:54
Hi Eileen
Last from me for this evening, I had another rummage for Strand-field and Trip Hall and bearing in mind Mathew Scanlan was of Loughill, I had a look round that parish on the map. I followed the shoreline and sure enough, or shore enough, I found an area not far from the church near Mount Trenchard (Spring Rice's place I think) called Strand-fields, on which stood Leahys Lodge or Leahys House. Not too far distant towards Loghill stood Hip Hall, and I think this might easily have been deciphered as Trip Hall from an old manuscript. Incredibly, a small part of it remains, though looks in utter ruin. The only ref I can find to Hip Hall is in - strangely enough - one of Gerald 'The Collegians' Griffin's letters, which I found in The Life of Gerald Griffin by his brother, in which a number of his letters were published (nice book, found two editions). In this book, Griffin wrote to his correspondent, identified as the mysterious 'L' (wasn't it all so shadowy!) 'I am come home only this evening, wearied from steering the Hip Hall boat'.

Griffin was indeed familiar with his subject. PS: I've always wondered about Griffin's title, do you think he was implying collegiates?

22 June 2012 19:26:49
Hello Jan
By now you know I wander. Have I found brother Anthony Scanlan? What do you think. Rebecca Scanlan appears to be in England too with a Wheeler niece.

23 June 2012 10:15:24
Hi Eileen
How strange you should look into Anthony because I did the same this morning, and I'm wondering, Lewis had Cpt Scanlan at Ballycahane in 1830s, could this have been Anthony? You've found he was born in Ireland and living in UK, and on a search I found a Cpt and Commander Anthony Scanlan Esq piloting the frigate ship Sussex for the Blackwall Line during the 1850s. It was also Anthony Scanlan Esq of Ballycahane who subscribed to Lewis. What do you think? Couple of other names I observed on another read through the legal docs in that book (p184): 1813 deed Catherine Cudmore widow of John Cudmore of Ballycahane Castle mentions George Leake, Rathkeale Abbey, Godfrey Massey, Ballywire, Co Tipp, John Crips of Fort Eliza, Elizabeth Helen Crips (nee Cudmore), Richard Smyth of Smythfield Esq, Elizabeth Scanlan spinster (presumably the daughter who married McCullough). The 1801 lease was made between Rt Hon Earl of Clare and Mathew Scanlan Esq I'm almost tempted to positively identify him as son of Michael (brother of John Fitzgibbon of the will) but something is stopping me.

23 June 2012 20:38:55
Jan
Commander Scanlan and Anthony Scanlan married to Isabella Scanlan one and same. I went back again after I found a death notice - more informative than death registers.One of the witnesses to his marriage could have been John Chadwick, an attorney, of Ballinard, Interesting that one of your Revs - Joseph C Armstrong married a Caroline Damer Chadwick of Ballinard. Ok I know I am going a long way around but it is a bit like sewing. I prefer the challenge of mending something rather than cutting out a pattern. First you have to unpick the seams to get to the part you need to repair. That's what I am doing – unpicking.

25 June 2012 09:13:38
Good morning Eileen

I disciplined myself to the Scanlan facts as we have them last night, ie, Ballycahane was leased to Michael Scanlan Esq of Ballynaha by the Earl of Clare 1787/8. Michael died Feb 1801. In this same year, Oct, the same 'estate' is leased by Mathew Scanlan of Loughill Esq from the Earl of Clare. Why Matthew? The eldest, Michael, had by then built Ballyknockane (1793/4), many of the other brothers were dead from military service. Mathew, 'son of Michael of Ballynaha' who died in 1840 is evidently son of Michael, and John Scanlan's father. The names of Matthew's sons, John, Michael, Francis - were those of his brothers (all excepting Anthony, a curious choice). Along the way we have discovered information about the other sons, Francis, who dropped dead in Limerick, Anthony, a captain (interesting that he was at sea from as early as 1835 on the Hellas), a daughter married a doctor, the only one we know nothing of is Michael. And so I think we have a strong enough case to name Matthew Scanlan of Ballynaha, Loughill, and Ballycahane, as his father. I loved the way you tracked down Rebekah Scanlan, right to her death in 1858. She was about 40 when she married JFS, so it was perhaps a keep-it-in-the-family marriage.

25 June 2012 10:49:31

One more interesting point Eileen about Gerald Griffin and that during his childhood his parents lived for some time at Fairy Lawn, until about 1817 when they emigrated, and I happened to notice the residence, Fairy Lawn, on the map yesterday, right beside Hip Hall. It makes sense of Mary Agnes Hickson's comment that his novel was seen in poor taste by the afflicted families.

25 June 2012 20:10:16

Hello Jan

Just back from seeing the Olympic Torch travel through D_____. It passed along the main road and there is a convenient footpath from here so I waved to dozens of policemen on flash motorbikes and then cheered the little boy in a wheelchair who was carrying the torch. I didn't qualify for a free bottle of Cola. So back to the real world. Sorry I disagree re Matthew being the father. I think it was Michael Scanlan Junior. Why? If we are to accept that John Scanlan's father died when John was young then that rules out Matthew (d1840). There were two Michaels, father and son. 1797 Michael Scanlan jnr of Ballynaha appointed High Sherrif Limerick. It was common to find the same person reappointed over the years but there is no mention of Michael Scanlan jnr after this date implying that he had died. Jan 1792 Miss Elizabeth Scanlan daughter of Michael Scanlan of Ballynaha marries Hon George Massey. Was it this influential marriage that got the job for Michael Scanlan jnr? Found online Michael Scanlan jnr witness at this marriage. June 1840 Matthew Scanlan, son of late Michael Scanlan of Ballynaha and brother in law to Hon George Eyre Massey dies. So Matthew is brother to Elizabeth Scanlan. Nov 1841 Constance Scanlan, youngest daughter of late Michael Scanlan and niece to Hon George Eyre Massey marries William Odell (and herein lies another tragic story - attached). So if Constance was niece then she is a generation later and sister to Michael Scanlan jnr? Oh dear just as it was in my mind working out I found William Scanlan and now got some niggles. The William Scanlan at Ballyknockane - lease renewed to him on Ballyknockane 1837. Do you have Lieutenant Connell (Colin) Scanlan, 39th foot, wounded Pyrenees died Bayonne Aug 1813? Never mind - read the William O'Dell story. Blames interbreeding!

26 June 2012 10:21:05
Hi Eileen
But only if we are to accept that his father died young; I'm working on the theory that his parents were alive. And what if Michael Scanlan jnr was no longer junior because HIS father had died? Mathew was also Michael's son, Elizabeth's brother, and Hon George Eyre Massey's brother-in-law. Mathew's son Francis (John's brother) who died 1869, was reported to be brother of John who was hanged; the other report that claimed he was a nephew doesn't fit. I was thinking about Francis; he never married, I wonder did he have a hard life, with the label of brother of the murderer? Did people shy of him because of this? It must have been a considerable burden to bear in those times. I was thinking that if I could find Mathew's grave there might be some info on the headstone. Also his wife, Catherine (Cudmore) Scanlan, when did she die and where was she buried? It could have been Ballycahane, or Ballingarry, where there is no doubt a family vault beneath the nettles, or even Kilpeacon. Biggest problem is lack of burial records. I've been to Ballingarry churchyard, the rear is just a wilderness, you can see the vaults and stones but the brambles are like trees and the ivy, oh the ivy. My theory that John Scanlan was probably born at Hip Hall, Loughill (Longhill, Loghill) can't be checked because baptism records start in 1812, but I'm going to try to track down some local history on Hip Hall. I must find that one more piece that I know eludes me, because I could of course be completely wrong on all this.

26 June 2012 17:22:03
Hello Jan
What a delight your Poor Man was to read! It spurs me on and am trying to work out the family tree that will show Elizabeth Scanlan and William O'Dell were cousins. It may give up more clues. If you want the full story of the murder and trial just shout. What a sad family the Scanlans were.

27 June 2012 15:11:18
Hi Eileen
Yes, it was a pretty sad and tragic case, you're right to say the Scanlans were a sad family, I'm sure had there been a descendant of John Scanlan an effort would have been made to redress his one-sided reputation. I feel the Scanlan storm slowly passing, and last night I went back to the church.

29 June 2012 22:15:36
Hi Eileen
Just home from Glin and washing down beans-on-toast with a cup of tea. It was and it wasn't a waste of time trip, because I collected my friend Nuala en route and we had a good old chat along the road there and back, plus tea and cakes. But the 'local history resources that can only be read in the library' consisted of one book of recollections published in 1996 that I am confident would be available in Killarney branch - in fact, I'm going to check now ... check in progress at borrowbooks ...But it doesn't really matter, because all I really wanted was a Scanlan association with Hip Hall to check my theory of Trip Hall, and in the above book I found one so I think a transcription error most likely. What I also found interesting was that nearby land on which was situate Fairy Lawn was leased by the Griffins (Collegians) from the Royse family, who were leasing from the owner of Carrowbane, the Protestant Bishop of Limerick. And interestingly, the bishop at this particular period was Charles Mongan Warburton, evidently rubbing shoulders with the Countess of Clare. Wasn't it a small pond. PS: yes, copy of book in my local library.

13 July 2012 11:40:22
Good morning Eileen
Had a very stressful day yesterday, went to Limerick straight from class and the sat nav had set an arrival time of half five. Fine, but it hadn't anticipated the accident or road works or whatever was causing the miles of traffic at Limerick turnoff. And so kept going, missed the next turn off, ended up in Ballina Co Tipperary, sent up country lanes and got caught in herds of cows etc etc, why does it always happen to me? Took me a while to find Dooradoyle library as it's sited in a large shopping centre but finally, at 7pm, was reading the Ballingarry records. One good thing is I found no record of 'our' Scanlans; lots of Ballyknockane and Kilbeg Scanlans, and a small number of Ballinahaha ones, mainly later dates.What the records have told me is that it would appear I don't need to venture into the undergrowth of Ballingarry churchyard. But the questions remain: where was Francis who died 1869 buried? Where were John Scanlan's parents buried, ie: where was Matthew Scanlan buried in 1840? The most logical answer I can come up with is Ballycahane parish church, if they were of Ballycahane House, or

perhaps Loughill (Hip Hall), Matthew Scanlan's former residence. I am going to chance my arm and contact the RCB to see if anything at all survives of the parish records.

07 August 2012 09:11:14
Hi Eileen
I thought I'd try one last time to find out what happened to John's brother Michael as we know about his other siblings – didn't find Michael, but found others.

08 August 2012 10:18:13
Hi Eileen
Hope all is well. I was looking through more Scanlan items last night and noted that Scanlan was said to have joined Chitty's 35th regiment at Cork and confirmed this regiment at Cork in an online book. Isn't it marvellous when all the pieces add up? What I also found was that the regiment's colonel died from rabies in 1819 after being bitten by a 'tame' fox and I further found that Cpt Chitty is mentioned in another memoir: An Eloquent Soldier, The Peninsular War Journals of Lieutenant Charles Crowe of the Inniskillings, 1812-1814' which brings me to my point, that your father's diaries, when you have them done, 'must' be published.

08 August 2012 17:04:56
Hello Jan
My attention has been taken a little by the Olympics but I think we have enough medals now☺ No joy with Catherine or Michael Scanlan but one of my onions for Dr David McCullagh although really it was not funny - but an onion nevertheless.

08 August 2012 22:12:10
Hi Eileen
I found another navy list today re: John Fitzgibbon Scanlan, that he was a 'cornet' in 1806, first lieutenant in 1812, half-pay 1814 and I think this must be a different JFS as surely too young to have enlisted at about age ten? And his brother-in-law claimed he was a second lieutenant of marines, not a first?

18 August 2012 16:31:42
Hi Eileen
Found ref to an 1862 article evidently by Lord Monteagle or a descendant of his who arrested Scanlan. Seems John Scanlan asked to speak to Monteagle (Spring Rice) in his cell and told him: Sullivan instead of putting her as he had agreed, on board an American vessel, stunned her with the

musket butt end, and then threw her into the Shannon. As a proof of the truth of my story you will find the musket hid in the cave under the promontory from whence the boat started'. Bearing in mind your items on illegal transportation at the time Eileen (Judith Lynch) Scanlan's instruction to put her on a vessel is entirely plausible. Isn't it tempting to go look for the musket☺

18 August 2012 18:59:08
Hi Eileen
Just thinking, the image commonly accepted to be that where John Scanlan lived cannot possibly be correct - and I fell into the same error - because Ballycahane House was burned down by rebels in 1822 and Scanlan had been dead for two years.

18 August 2012 20:47:42
Hello Jan
Just a line I am trying and will work on tomorrow. It would appear a Samuel Lover painted quite a famous watercolour - exhibited at the Royal Hibernian Society in 1841, The Colleen Bawn and Colleen Dhu. I reckon this painting inspired the name for Ellen Hanly. Now real culture - X factor.

19 August 2012 18:24:41
Hi Eileen
The smallness of the circle is reinforced when assembling the docs. Remember our abducted Judith, well I happened to come across Clare View on the map which is situated by the river Shannon (surprise surprise) and is still there, as is the gate lodge. It is located close to Ballydonohoe House near Glin and Tarbert. I also had another search of Manister, because Ballycahane was part of this area too, and via this I found a Thomas H Royse of Rathkeale and the name rang a big bell, because Royce (Royse) was the principal landlord of Hip Hall and Fairy Lawn, and on another related document I found all the same little circle, Royse, Odell, Massy, etc. I also have one last theory on Michael Scanlan, John's brother, I went back to a doc I looked at once before, the death of an Ellen Scanlan of Thomondgate, Limerick, wife of Michael Scanlan. She is referred to as mother of Bartholomew Scanlan reporter for the Limerick Chronicle. I found a death notice for Bartholomew Scanlan in 1859, and he must have been of some importance if you read the notice I'm attaching. What I'm saying is, could Michael and Ellen Scanlan, parents of Bartholomew, have been the missing Michael? I need a break☹ I'm almost delirious.

19 August 2012 18:24:45
Hello Jan

Enclosed will answer 99% of your queries. But although I can date The Colleen Bawn, The true history of Ellen Hanly, I cannot find anything to attribute it to Rev Richard Fitzgerald. He would have been born 1801 and would have been 19 at the time? I did see that he was friendly with Spring Rice. Nothing shows of any literary skills.

19 August 2012 18:33:29
Hi Eileen
Look forward to going through all that after dinner, with a glass of wine! I have notes somewhere that he was served with a writ for deception on his deathbed.

20 August 2012 00:04:45
Hi Eileen
I did love your Boucicault item, and that he fell trying to save the colleen from drowning. I also smiled when I read that Fitzgerald died at Ballydonohoe House - he was no less than a neighbour of Clare View. And a near neighbour of Hip Hall. Oh what a small place it was! And how neighbourly they all were towards one another in literature!

20 August 2012 10:40:50
Good morning Eileen
I was wondering where the ref I found to Lord Monteagle's account of the case came from, and a search (oh the wonders of the internet) just revealed the source, an 1868 publication by Nassau William Senior. We have a new name - De Lacy. I wonder were the Cudmore Crips linked to this family in a roundabout way?

20 August 2012 10:57:53
Hi Eileen
Mary Charlotte Mair Simpson (1825-1907), just downloaded and read through a book she wrote, Many Memories of Many People, in which she included Trench and Lord Monteagle, though didn't go into detail as Senior did. But from what I can see, by strange coincidence, she seems to have been Nassau William Senior's daughter. Hardly a thing to be had about her online, apart from a number of publications.

20 August 2012 11:33:07
Hi Eileen
Just had a quick look around and found this in Lewis entry for Ballingarry: A building called the Turret was erected by a branch of the De Lacy family and repaired by Col. O'Dell in 1683, as appears by a stone in the chimney; it

was lately the residence of Major O'Dell. Is this enough indication of a family connection?

20 August 2012 17:32:27
Hello Jan
Your succession of short emails was almost like listening to you thinking. Some answers here maybe. The Turrett file is simply because I like a new name. I was reading about Samuel Lover (Colleen Bawn /Colleen Dhu) I didn't realise what a famous man he was - had connections to Bouccicault too.

21 August 2012 10:27:17
Hi Eileen
Listening to me think - now that is scary. Laughed at the duelling stories from Jackson's Turret, especially the discrepancy in names, Lloyd/Taylor - or perhaps there were two duels fought that day. Though it was hardly funny, the victim's child born the day he died. And Sir William Spring's estate - but not title - going to his sisters, one a Mrs Discipline, from Bury - I wonder did she adhere to this after the windfall? I had a re-think on De Lacy. Senior was quite specific that she was a De Lacy. Do you think it possible that John Scanlan's mother, Catherine Cudmore, whose father was John Cudmore Esq, might have had a mother named De Lacy? This of course is reaching back into the late eighteenth century.

21 August 2012 13:07:48
Hi Eileen
From what I've been able to find online, it seems the Lacy, or de Lacy family was historically intimately connected with Limerick notably in Bruff and Ballingarry. Read that 'though the name is still found in Co. Limerick and other parts of Munster, the ancestral estates of the de Lacys, which were at Ballingarry, Bruff and Bruree, have long since passed into other hands, and even a century ago there was no large landed proprietor of the name in Ireland'. Most other items I've found relate to General Maurice de Lacy (died 1820) and Count Peter de Lacy. It seems this might be too hard a nut to crack.

21 August 2012 16:49:20
Hello Jan
Just a few scraps but I like the first one best. Was it our Michael Scanlan and why was he duelling? Also enclosed Spring of Mount Spring just in case they are of use.

22 August 2012 11:15:59
Dear Eileen
Your Rice doc illustrates how important it was to get your religion right in the 1700s, especially before you died. Started on the introduction last night, it's just like piecing together a jigsaw.

22 August 2012 14:05:15
Dear Eileen
Just editing our 'Scanlan' mails and it's handy to look back at what we've done. Some time back we had mention of a Rev William Massy of Glenwilliam Castle, Co Limerick who it seems died in 1822. He was a prebend of Dysart and rector of Clonbeg, apparently. It seems he married a Scanlan of 'Ballinaher' who was a daughter of Michael. Another promising looking Massy/Scanlan link in this puzzle. Married four times it seems, but can you verify any of this?

23 August 2012 10:55:12
Good morning Eileen
Worked late into the night, hardly worth going to bed, but have the first draft just about completed. This morning in the shower I decided to try to find out about the journalist who named John Fitzgibbon Scanlan, though I doubted it could be done with so common a name: How wrong! He was an American professor of English who lived for many years in Dublin researching Irish history and novelists including of course Griffin. No wonder he was in the know. He contributed a few articles to the Irish press in the 1960s.

23 August 2012 11:27:36
Jan
Just bought the Flanagan triology on Ebay. Total cost incl. postage £6.47 - not bad!

23 August 2012 13:21:06
Hi Eileen
Just spectacularly failed my test. It's important to blame others when these things happen, so I'm pointing the finger directly at the dead - and today, it's Thomas Flanagan! Ps: My purple socks with red hat and pink ribbon didn't work today☺

23 August 2012 14:26:41
So sorry Jan - all those boring classes! May I join you on the thicko list please - Triology?

24 August 2012 10:30:19
Hi Eileen
There's nothing wrong with a triology. In fact, from what I can see online, it might be the archaic version, the more inferior version used by the commoners. Hope to get intro to you before weekend is out.

26 August 2012 23:13:20
Hi Eileen
What an unusually quiet weekend I've had, but a quiet house means I get things done. Attach first draft, I must still add a paragraph about John's life but am too tired to think any more this eve. Also found another version of the arrest which claimed he was apprehended at the residence of Mr M___ of S___ perhaps Massey of Stagdale Lodge. Sent me off course for a few hours, but back on track.

27 August 2012 16:33:42
Hello Jan
I am delighted that you are using that wonderful painting as your cover. I just gaze at it and dream! I couldn't find anything more on John Scanlan's youth but enclose a couple of snippets for Baal's Bridge. How the same names crop up.

28 August 2012 09:55:32
Hi Eileen
Very interesting items on Baals Bridge, especially the early date, 1361, of Sir John de Galwey's defence of it. Perhaps this explains why Scanlan's horses wouldn't cross it, it must have been very rickety by that stage☺ After struggling to add the final paragraph about John, it finally occurred to me that of course I can't do this, because nothing is known of him - the object of our exercise! And so I added a paragraph late last night saying just that, and it's done. A week or so ago I asked Peter if he would read over it when written, but didn't hear back. Just had a mail from him to say that his dear mother passed away just after that mail arrived.

28 August 2012 13:06:03
Hi Eileen
It occurred to me that I don't really need to lay this up, as there are no images, etc, so I can just upload as a document - see attached. Larger than anticipated. I've just been looking at J Egerton Wilkes, who produced Eily O'Connor 1831, but can't find much and wonder, could J Egerton Wilkes have been the dramatist I found in an 1891 book of the life and reminiscences of Edward Leman Blanchard, whose 'chum' was Thomas Egerton Wilks? A footnote states of Wilks: 'Died this day [29 Sept 1854] in

a state of wretched poverty. His first work was a romantic drama, The Red Cross, produced at Sadler's Wells in 1831 and he afterwards wrote some 200 plays'. If this is the same man Eileen, Eily would have been one of his earliest plays.

28 August 2012 18:34:33
Of course you are right Jan☺. I see from the ad in 1831 the name was J. Egerton Wilks. Thereafter it is either Mr Egerton Wilks or Thomas Egerton Wilks. Maybe, as it was one of his first works, the Press did not know of him. Was Egerton Wilks his real name? I cannot find him either in the census. You'll see from a court case (Boucicault) that he had sold the rights to some of his works some years preceding his death. Why? Now that's another story ☺.

29 August 2012 12:13:05
Hi Eileen
The 1860 Boucicault vs Egan case, did Mr Egan also produce a version of The Colleen Bawn?

29 August 2012 15:27:12
Hello Jan
Mr Egan is another mystery for some date in the future, a long, long way into the future! It would appear that he is (In 1851 census) Frederick Egan b. 1819 occupation Tragedian. The strange thing is that there is no trace of any of them after or before that date. So no, he wasn't a dramatist - maybe just a chancer?

30 August 2012 11:00:30
Hi Eileen
How I love a chancer! I've had a look at Frederick Bailey Egan this morning, also known as 'Barney' Egan in theatre circles, and 'fond of a practical joke'. He is mentioned in a number of theatrical memoirs and in an article on the theatre in Gentleman's Magazine in 1886, described by John Coleman as 'late', as well as 'the handsomest man I have ever seen'. He was an actor at the Royal Adelphi, Wigan c1850s/50s, and described also as a comedian before he took up stage management. Found his daughter Rose, (Mrs Bishop) made her stage debut in 1873. So Egan was sued by Boucicault for staging, or attempting to stage, another version of Colleen Bawn written by 'Horsman'. I found a death notice for a Charles Horsman, who died in great poverty in 1886, I wonder was it the same man? I wonder how many ‘pirate’ copies of Colleen Bawn were in circulation.

30 August 2012 16:32:57
Hello Jan
To give you a smile - read the first article in enclosed:) Then I found a letter to The Era from Charles Horsman re The Colleen Bawn. May be useful.

31 August 2012 11:11:46
Hi Eileen
May be useful! You've opened up another bag of delights.

01 September 2012 21:20:12
Hi Eileen
One last query: Kathleen Mavourneen or St Patrick's Eve, attributed to William Travers, 'could' be based on the Colleen. I wonder can you do better than 'could'?

02 September 2012 11:23:26
Hello Jan
Found death announcement of William Travers - no doubt he was the author of Kathleen Mavoureen - backed up by several advertisements. His real name was William Pope. There was a much earlier military play, St Patrick's Eve, but nothing to do with Kathleen Mavoureen. Just for interest enclosed this too. I wonder if actor Bill Travers is a descendant?

03 September 2012 10:42:17
Good morning Eileen
I was wondering about St Patrick's Eve, and thought perhaps it was styled in this way because Scanlan was hanged on St Patrick's Eve but clearly there was an earlier play. William Travers Pope wrote more than 100 dramas and his Colleen play, one of his earliest, helped to establish his reputation in the East End.

11 September 2012 19:00:19
Hi Eileen
Off to Shannon at five this morning in the dark and rain and then a u-turn and back again. Ryan couldn't face boarding, Thomas Flanagan's Irish Novelists was waiting. In his section on Griffin, he seems to have concentrated on Griffin's handling of the content etc rather than the content itself. I could find no suggestion of how he knew Fitzgibbon, he has just repeated the well-worn storyline. It must have thrown up during his research, but he deemed it not relevant to his purpose. A couple of things I found interesting: Lydia Jane Leadbeater Fisher – remember her? She was a married neighbour of Griffin in Limerick, and this is what Flanagan wrote: 'beyond any doubt, Lydia and Griffin were deeply in love ... because it

existed in such strained and hopeless circumstances, makes several of the letters painful to read'. This was in 1829; by 1832, 'he was anxious to end his relationship with Lydia'. In another of Griffin's books, he focussed on the smuggling trade which brings us right back to Poor Man's Daughter.

11 September 2012 21:11:38
Hello Jan
The Aylmers seem to be another tragic family. Some of them died in a dreadful train crash in Wales whilst travelling to Ireland then in later years the two surviving sons were caught up in the Boer war.

12 September 2012 09:19:27
Hi Eileen
Flanagan mentioned a new name, 'Curran', I went hunting, and found this: Sketches of The Irish Bar (1825) by Sheil and Sketches of The Irish Bar by Curran Esq (1825) ☺ Don't scream yet! It seems both wrote for The New Monthly, and the account was attributed to Sheil in 1854 and Curran in 1855. So who wrote it? Lady Morgan: 'We [her and Curran] talked of the good but coarse Irish novel, The Collegians ... the whole melancholy event was given by Curran in the New Monthly Magazine'. Well at least it was according to Curran☺ who would seem to be William Henry, son of John Philpot. Lady Morgan describes Scanlan as dissipated, all meanings could be applied to him: foolish, drunk, broke, runaway. Lady Morgan summed-up from her armchair (bit like us from our computers) that Scanlan was guilty. Anyway, checking the uncle/nephew ref, your list of dates gave names returned to serve as Sheriff in 1829, including "Limerick, William Scanlan of Ballineha, Esq". Check☺ (it made me smile when I read that this William (Odell) Scanlan married his cousin, daughter of Cpt John Brown of Clonboy and Bridgetown, who was widow of James Fisher of Limerick and that their son, Michael, married Hannah-Jane, daughter of James J Fisher Esq of Limerick and his wife Lydia-Jane☺).

12 September 2012 15:16:39
Hi Eileen
Checking a Griffin reference on your Aylmer doc, and ended up on ricorso. I wondered who was behind it, & decided to have 'a quick look'. Two hours later, after much internet pursuit, I tracked the author (Dr) to the University of U_____, and have had a very pleasant time looking at some of his publications, like James Joyce in the OUP VIP series (number eleven), Becket and Beyond 'waiting for something' and perhaps too, A Disorderly Girl in 1980 (read the plot but sounds too complicated). No wonder I get so little done ...

www.ingramcontent.com/pod-product-compliance
Ingram Content Group UK Ltd.
Pitfield, Milton Keynes, MK11 3LW, UK
UKHW020234250726
13967UKWH00001B/352